Courthouses of the Commonwealth

Photographs by George Peet and Gabrielle Keller

Edited with a Preface by Robert J. Brink

The University of Massachusetts Press

Amherst, 1984

Library of Congress Cataloging in Publication Data
Peet, George, 1946–
Courthouses of the commonwealth.
1. Court-houses—Massachusetts. I. Keller,
Gabrielle, 1952– . II. Brink, Robert J.,
1950– . III. Title.
NA 4472.M3P4   1984   725'.15'09744   84–8752
ISBN 0–87023–438–2
ISBN 0–87023–439–0 (pbk.)

Contents

Foreword

THE courthouses of Massachusetts are a truly remarkable collection of public buildings that vary considerably in age, present use and utility, physical condition, architectural style, and historical significance. They range from still-used buildings nearly two centuries old to ultramodern facilities of a far more recent vintage. In some instances, examples of both stand nearly side by side as contrasting markers of the Commonwealth's legal history.

Our courthouses are monuments to our legal tradition, its noble purposes and occasional tragic miscarriages. They evoke the memory of historical events and of the aspirations, frustrations, and fears of the many people—the learned, the dedicated, the articulate, the oppressed and despised, the avaricious and the brutal—whom the law has summoned to exercise their skills or to account for their actions. Our courthouses are the arenas for the resolution of social and economic problems reduced to their most intimate level, a case or controversy. They are theaters for high drama and objective symbols of our guaranteed freedoms. They are also the repository of those records that, in specifically personal terms, trace the evolution of our society and system of government from colonial times to the present.

The magnificent photographs in this volume capture, in their essence, these many aspects of our courthouses. In their beauty, these photographs transcend a cold study of architectural types and period furnishings. Instead, they instill an intrinsic sense of the purpose for which these structures were built. In them, the courthouses have taken on a derivatively human aspect. They are not merely buildings, rooms, and furniture but are, rather, monuments that evoke several centuries of human effort and progress.

The photographs in this volume allow those of us who regularly attend courthouses to take a more appreciative view than our labors ordinarily permit. One cannot peruse this book without being compelled to reflect, not only upon the efforts of our predecessors to establish and to observe the rule of law, but also upon their attempts to embody adherence to that rule in architectural form. For this respite and opportunity for reflection, we owe a debt of gratitude to the Trustees of the Social Law Library and to the photographers, George Peet and Gabrielle Keller.

Honorable Edward F. Hennessey
Chief Justice
Supreme Judicial Court

Preface

We require from buildings, as from men, two kinds of goodness: first, the doing of their practical duty well: then that they be graceful and pleasing in doing it; which last is itself another form of duty.
—RUSKIN, *Stones of Venice*

O N behalf of the Trustees of the Social Law Library and its librarian, Edgar J. Bellefontaine, I am pleased to present this study of the courthouses of Massachusetts. Brilliantly photographed by George Peet and Gabrielle Keller with an essay by architect and historian John C. McConnell, the work surveys each of the state's Superior Court facilities currently in use. Reflecting their county origins, these buildings also frequently house local probate courts, registries of deeds, and offices of county commissioners. And the Suffolk County Courthouse complex, which combines the original 1895 structure with a tall twentieth-century addition, is the seat of the state's highest appellate tribunals, the city's municipal and housing courts as well as the Social Law Library.

Although it is no longer in use and was never a Superior Court facility in the modern sense of the term, the Old Plymouth County Courthouse (pl. 60) is included in this volume for its historical significance as the oldest courthouse in Massachusetts. Constructed in 1749, its architect is purported to have been Peter Oliver, the last Royal Chief Justice of the Superior Court of Judicature. In the midst of Revolutionary turmoil, Oliver accepted a salary grant from the Crown rather than the colonial legislature, an act that resulted in threats of impeachment. Although Loyalist Governor Thomas Hutchinson successfully thwarted those proceedings, hostile jurors throughout the province nonetheless prevented Oliver from sitting as a judge by refusing to serve on cases over which he presided. The threat of mob violence even prevented him from ever again sitting in this courthouse in the county of his residence—a residence that he soon abandoned when he fled this country.

The book also pictures the Old State House (pl. 61) which stands, between Court Street and State Street in downtown Boston, in stark contrast to the high-rise buildings that now surround it. During much of the colonial period it was the seat of the Superior Court of Judicature—the predecessor of today's Supreme Judicial Court. Royal judges were arrayed, as John Adams once described them, in their "rich robes of English broadcloth; in their large cambric bands and immence judicial wigs." It was before those judges that Adams put aside his own political sentiments to defend with all his skill the hated British soldiers accused of shooting unarmed civilians in the Boston Massacre. Rising above personal politics, he at that moment personified the most noble of human ideals, the ideal of impartial justice that lies at the heart of the law.

Other people, in other courtrooms, have also pursued that ideal; and the courthouses of the Commonwealth, constructed for the most part in the nineteenth century by an independent people proud of their freedom, were intended as settings in which free citizens could do their public duty in an architecture that enhanced respect for the law and inspired aesthetic admiration. Indeed, many Massachusetts courthouses were built as grand monuments to justice, with vast

The Social Law Library, Boston Courthouse, Suffolk County

open spaces, cavernous domes, and sweeping staircases, while the majesty of the courtrooms themselves was intended to mirror the majesty of the law.

Very early in the documentary process it became paradoxically clear that many of the older buildings had decayed and the decorum of the courts did not mirror the outmoded romantic imagery. A court system plagued by twentieth-century problems burdens many of these nineteenth-century buildings.

Indeed, there have been mounting criticisms of the state's many aged courthouses. Of the twenty-five Superior and probate court facilities still in use, nineteen were built before the turn of the century. Inadequate space for court personnel, clerical functions, and record storage is a common lament of judicial administrators trying to cope with the litigation explosion. Plumbing and electrical systems are often outdated. Heating is frequently inadequate and air-conditioning is almost nonexistent. The long and difficult transformation of the court system from one administered by the counties to a unified state system has even deferred day-to-day maintenance. As this Preface is being written, the General Court is considering legislation that would require the state to assume responsibility for some of these buildings traditionally owned and maintained by the counties.

In selecting images to include in this volume there was a decision to refocus attention upon the architectural beauty of the older buildings, although not to the complete exclusion of the disrepair that has tarnished the dignity of the courts. It is hoped that by highlighting the architectural merits of the courthouses, the book will promote enlightened preservation of the structures themselves, even if they are put to uses other than that of serving the administration of justice.

Publication of *Courthouses of the Commonwealth* is the consummation of a project that involved the help of many people. First and foremost is Frederick H. Norton, Jr., who recently retired as executive secretary of the Boston Bar Association after twenty-six years of devoted service. Recognizing the quality of the photographs, he featured them as a continuing cover series for the *Boston Bar Journal* through much of 1981 and 1982. Responses to the series were extremely enthusiastic, so much so that the Social Law Library was encouraged to pursue a more extensive public exhibition. With the support of the Boston Bar Association, an exhibit was mounted at the Newbury Street art gallery of the Boston Architectural Center.

The exposure generated from both this exhibition and a "Courthouses of the Commonwealth" poster printed in conjunction with it helped enlist the support of experts in the fields of art, architecture, and photography to attest to the value of a book project. A special expression of appreciation is due Clifford S. Ackley, Associate Curator of Prints, Drawings, and Photographs at the Boston Museum of Fine Arts, David S. Gillespie, Northeast Regional Director of the National Trust for Historic Preservation, and David Ulrich of the Art Institute of Boston. Their letters were instrumental in securing the financial support necessary to publish the volume.

Generous grants from the following organizations were secured to help fund production costs, especially to ensure that the quality of the reproduction was faithful to that of the original prints: the Charles H. Cross Charitable Foundation, the David Greenewalt Charitable Trust, Lawyers Weekly Publications, the Massachusetts Bar Foundation, the State Street Bank and Trust Company, and the Emma and John Quint Memorial Fund.

An expression of personal gratitude is due John J. Roche and George H. Foley, partners at the Boston law firm of Hale and Dorr and co-trustees of the Emma and John Quint Memorial Fund. Through a series of timely grants, they helped underwrite not only the printing of this volume, but also the printing of the poster alluded to earlier, as well as the travel expenses of the photographers as they crisscrossed the Commonwealth.

The photographers, George Peet and Gabrielle Keller, traveled to each of the state's fourteen counties, and at every courthouse represented in this work they received a warm welcome from judges, clerks of court, and county officials who opened the doors to courtrooms, offices, and even private lobbies.

From the Old Plymouth County Courthouse built in 1749 to the newest of facilities, the courthouses of the Commonwealth form an exceptional "textbook" of American courthouse architecture. We are indebted to architect and historian John C. McConnell for his detailed essay examining this heritage.

Old or new, in repair or disrepair, the courthouses of the Commonwealth stand as symbols of our attitudes about law and as monuments to our legal tradition. The photographs featured in this volume eloquently document this legacy.

Robert J. Brink
Social Law Library
Boston

1 Plymouth Courthouse, Plymouth County

2 Boston Courthouse, Suffolk County

3   Taunton Courthouse, Bristol County

4   Taunton Courthouse, Bristol County

5   Salem Courthouse, Essex County

6   Lawrence Courthouse, Essex County

7   Fitchburg Courthouse, Worcester County

8   Lowell Courthouse, Middlesex County

9   Lowell Courthouse, Middlesex County

10   Worcester Courthouse, Worcester County

11 Plymouth Courthouse, Plymouth County

12   Salem Courthouse, Essex County

13   Worcester Courthouse, Worcester County

14   Newburyport Courthouse, Essex County

15 Northampton Courthouse, Hampshire County

16   Northampton Courthouse, Hampshire County

17 New Bedford Courthouse, Bristol County

18   Cambridge Courthouse, Middlesex County

19 Barnstable Courthouse, Barnstable County

20 Barnstable Courthouse, Barnstable County

21   Worcester Courthouse, Worcester County

22   Worcester Courthouse, Worcester County

23   Worcester Courthouse, Worcester County

24   Greenfield Courthouse, Franklin County

25   Greenfield Courthouse, Franklin County

26   Lawrence Courthouse, Essex County

27 Lawrence Courthouse, Essex County

28   Lawrence Courthouse, Essex County (awaiting renovation)

29   Lawrence Courthouse, Essex County (awaiting renovation)

30 Northampton Courthouse, Hampshire County

31   Northampton Courthouse, Hampshire County

32 Northampton Courthouse, Hampshire County

33 Northampton Courthouse, Hampshire County

34   Northampton Courthouse, Hampshire County

35   Fitchburg Courthouse, Worcester County

36   Fitchburg Courthouse, Worcester County

37   Fitchburg Courthouse, Worcester County

38   Fitchburg Courthouse, Worcester County

39   Newburyport Courthouse, Essex County

40 Newburyport Courthouse, Essex County

41   Dedham Courthouse, Norfolk County

42   Dedham Courthouse, Norfolk County

43   Dedham Courthouse, Norfolk County

44 Dedham Courthouse, Norfolk County

45   Edgartown Courthouse, Dukes County

46   Edgartown Courthouse, Dukes County

47   Cambridge Courthouse, Middlesex County (under renovation)

48   Cambridge Courthouse, Middlesex County (under renovation)

49   Cambridge Courthouse, Middlesex County (under renovation)

50   Taunton Courthouse, Bristol County

51   Taunton Courthouse, Bristol County

52   Taunton Courthouse, Bristol County (old holding cell)

53   Taunton Courthouse, Bristol County (old prisoner facility)

54   Taunton Courthouse, Bristol County

55 Taunton Courthouse, Bristol County

56 Springfield Courthouse, Hampden County

57 Springfield Courthouse, Hampden County

58 Nantucket Courthouse, Nantucket County

59   Brockton Courthouse, Plymouth County

60   "Old Plymouth Courthouse," Plymouth County

61 "Old State House," Boston, Suffolk County

62   Boston Courthouse, Suffolk County

63   Boston Courthouse, Suffolk County

64   Supreme Judicial Court, Boston Courthouse, Suffolk County

65   Conference Room, Supreme Judicial Court, Boston Courthouse, Suffolk County

66   Pittsfield Courthouse, Berkshire County

67   Pittsfield Courthouse, Berkshire County

68   Lowell Courthouse, Middlesex County

69 Lowell Courthouse, Middlesex County

70   Lowell Courthouse, Middlesex County (unused rooms)

71 Lowell Courthouse, Middlesex County (unused rooms)

72   Lowell Courthouse, Middlesex County (unused rooms)

73   Lowell Courthouse, Middlesex County (unused rooms)

74 Salem Courthouse, Essex County

75 Salem Courthouse, Essex County

76   Salem Courthouse, Essex County

77　Fall River Courthouse, Bristol County

78   Plymouth Courthouse, Plymouth County

79   Plymouth Courthouse, Plymouth County

The Houses of the Law

A History of Superior
Court Architecture
in Massachusetts

John C. McConnell

Introduction

*We shape our buildings and they
shape us.*
—WINSTON CHURCHILL

IN America, notions of justice underpin our national identity so deeply that they have practically become part of the "genetic code" of American society—a sort of national protoplasm out of which arise all sorts of appeals to our common notions about national life. It was largely a perceived subversion of justice that catalyzed our movement to self-government, and we have spent all the years since the Declaration trying to define justice. But we are nonetheless rooted in the notion of justice for all. In the great fundamental and largely unconscious body of national emotion are found the manifestations by which our Great National Ideas, such as justice, are popularized and disseminated: in our sacred documents; our folktales, slogans, and highfalutin credos. Found there, too, are elements of a popular iconography—symbols and images in the mind's eye—which represent these great ideas.

The blindfolded woman with scales and sword certainly is one such icon, but there are others, more subtle, which involve buildings —imaginary courthouses or parts of them. It is these images of great columns, staircases, polished corridors, statuary, and the like, that are also the embodiment of justice for us. By remembering architectural forms in association with ideas about justice (or, say, God or corporate power) we create archetypes—physical forms that have meanings defined by their associational value. The courthouse itself is an archetypal form. The image of a courthouse in a shady square at the center of town is practically a complete metaphor for a typical American community, a potent icon that is central to our shared beliefs about ourselves.

All this applies to us in New England, because we are Americans, and yet seldom is New England considered typical of America. Generally, the shiretowns of Massachusetts are not typical American towns, but each shares something of a New England regional character—which includes a tolerance for individuality. And it is this, above other New England traits, that has blessed us with diversity in all things, including architecture. Massachusetts is practically unique among the states in having a body of Superior courthouses so diverse that almost every major period in American architectural history is represented. These buidings are truly a treat for those who wish to read in them statements about our past and about our efforts to set in our midst incarnations of ideas about justice. It is architecture that embodies law, houses those who administer it, and serves as a metaphor for its power and legitimacy.

Architecture, as much as law, deals with institutions and the relationship of individuals to them. Buildings can accommodate or thwart us. They direct and confound us; protect, threaten, elevate, humble, bore, amuse, or awe us. And they come laden with values that affect the ways we conduct ourselves and our opinions about the conduct of others. We also expect from architecture a kind of order that unifies the parts of experience that work better together, and separates those that work better in isolation; that defines our public and private spaces adequately; and that draws true distinctions between that which is special and important in our midst and that which is ordinary.

This book isolates the buildings where we have housed the administering of justice, and thereby offers an opportunity to examine a succession of changes in architectural conventions that have occurred in the making of courthouses. Accordingly, we expect in any given period to find evidence of certain standards that make courthouses *like* each other and *unlike* other building types.

First, they must speak to society about justice and the law. They should say "We are a *just* society."

Second, they are public governmental buildings in a democratic state, and should evince the democratic notion of access for all. They should say "We are a *democratic* people."

Third, they should make the process of justice seem to be one of the highest purposes of society, by being presented as monuments— as buildings of great social stature. They should say "I am a *monument* to justice."

Fourth, they should focus on a special theatrical space, the *courtroom*, as the unequivocal center of the drama of deciding what is just.

Finally, they should share with all other buildings of whatever function the recognition of the individual human being, respecting both physical size and spiritual uniqueness. They should say "We are a *humane* culture."

The Colonial Period

A new civilization was being born less out of plans and purposes than out of the unsettlement which the New World brought to the ways of the Old.
—DANIEL BOORSTIN

Both American architecture and American law share a common ancestry. To a large extent the entire construct of the American legal system is founded on English common law. It is our inherited tradition. In New England, the same can be said of our architectural history. We would not say today that either our law or architecture conspicuously resembles its English counterpart, but for the most part our early architecture was consciously English. In fact, it was generally as English as it could be, under the circumstances. Particularly in Massachusetts, our colonial foundations were predominantly British: the British sovereigns were our sovereigns; the language, currency, customs, laws, arts, and God were ours as well. And, although to a lesser extent than the first white Virginians, the first impulse of the English settlers of Massachusetts Bay (after sheer survival) was to lessen the profound sense of isolation in an incomprehensibly vast wilderness by making as complete a facsimile as possible of the England they had just left. To be sure, they intended to do England one better in *New* England; otherwise, they would have remained at home. But the world they fashioned for themselves remained, despite their most English efforts, intractably American.

Both the legal system and the architectural corpus generated by early Americans were almost exclusively brought about by practitioners who had no training in those fields—Puritan divines, merchants, men of general education in the case of the law, and carpenters, shipwrights, or "gentlemen practitioners" in the case of architecture. They operated on their sometimes dim memory of how things had been in England, and this memory was supplanted by new American conditions of climate, geography, scale, the theocratic Puritan polity, and their own opinions of how things ought to be. America inflected their remembered traditions and rendered them a unique reincarnation of English culture.

The New England building material was wood, and it has since become The American Material. Centuries before the settlement of America, however, the English countryside had been largely deforested and wood had become a relatively scarce commodity. Nevertheless, New England settlers had come from rural counties which still retained a wood vernacular architecture developed in the Middle Ages, and the carpenters among them knew that tradition well. Their first permanent houses closely resembled the heavy-timber framed homes with steeply pitched roofs they had left behind. These English medieval buildings must have provided early colonials with a measure of comfort, reassuring them that, though they were on the fringes of a remote and hostile continent, they were yet part of civilized England.

If the heavy frames of their early houses were, as was the practice in England, infilled with twig basketry and mud (wattle and daub), this practice did not last long. New England temperatures fluctuate much more than they do in Britain, and the wattle and daub, expanding and contracting with those changes in temperature, fell out. While clapboard siding is not unknown in England, it became the ubiquitous solution to the problem of providing an elastic membrane with which to cover New England buildings. This lent a characteristic thinness and unsubstantiality to these First Period houses—unpainted and drawn together around the meetinghouse and common of every town in the colony. The archetypal image of American building, the plain and foursquare wooden box with its tightly drawn wooden skin, dates from the earliest settlement of New England.

Most of the buildings of seventeenth-century New England were wooden-box houses, and their diamond-paned casement windows, overhanging upper stories, steeply pitched roofs, and tall pointed dormers were all elements of an English medieval vernacular building tradition. The universality and practicality of the wooden box in America was reinforced, starting around 1690, when buildings in the seventy-year-old colony began to exhibit marked stylistic change. Through this and all subsequent periods the basic wooden box has proven itself the capable bearer of any style devised, and Americans have been content to use the wooden box for all purposes and to think of style as an appliqué, "superadded," in the words of John Ruskin, "to utility."

In an effort to keep up with cultural developments in England, prosperous merchants in Boston at the dawn of the eighteenth century began putting up shops and houses, in brick as well as wood, with overt stylistic elements as part of their design. These elements were Classical—that is, they were architectural "words" (columns, cornices, balustrades, pediments) from an architectural "language" first developed in ancient Greece and Rome, the Classical cultures of antiquity. These Classical traditions had been revived first during the Renaissance in Italy around 1400, whence they spread across the European continent, coming last to England around 1600 under the aegis of the great architect Inigo Jones (1573–1652). Meanwhile in Italy, the principles of structural clarity and pure harmonics of correct proportions characteristic of Renaissance architecture were being transformed, partly as the architectural embodiment of the Counter-Reformation, into the sensual delight of exuberantly curvaceous solids and voids of a new Classicism, the Baroque. This, in turn, reached England around 1650. It can be argued that the best English Baroque work was that of Sir Christopher Wren (1632–1723), the architect of St. Paul's Cathedral and some fifty-one London city churches, all rebuilt after the destruction of that city by fire in 1666. The great Wren was so lionized at home and in the colonies that to this day countless American buildings are ascribed to him, although there is no documentation (and very little likelihood) of his ever having designed a colonial building.

It was the influence of Wren and his followers (notably James Gibbs) in England that was most profoundly felt in the colonies, transmitted by men arriving with firsthand knowledge of London's new buildings, as well as numerous architectural publications of up-to-the-minute designs. These books depicted an architecture commonly known as "Georgian," although this designation (as with "Victorian") is not properly a style at all but rather the name of an age corresponding to the reign of British monarchs. Georgian architecture was an assortment of several styles using a Classical vocabulary, one of which has been called Wren/Baroque.

The Old Plymouth Courthouse (pl. 60) is a provincial example of this style, although its most salient characteristic is not stylistic at all, but rather that it is obviously a simple wooden box with a thin wooden skin stretched tightly around its framing members. It is also virtually indistinguishable from houses of the same era—it is quite literally a court "house." But unlike typical First Period houses, it is white; its doors and windows are symmetrically disposed across its façades, it has no dormers, and its roof has a shallow pitch. And its style-giving elements are all derived from the Classical language of architecture: a cornice at the eaves of the roof and in the triangular pedimented end gable; small Classical entablatures at the heads of the first-floor windows (double hung, now, rather than old-fashioned casements); and, of course, the front door with its elaborate Classical surround, which is the most characteristic feature of American Wren/Baroque buildings.

As had been typical of early colonial public structures, the Plymouth Court shared this building with a market on the lower story and town offices on the first floor. The courtroom was the entire second floor, and traces of its original vaulted plaster ceiling remain. The judge presided from a raised desk, with a lower clerk's desk immediately in front, which was flanked by boxes for the sheriff and court crier. Counsel faced the judge; behind them sat the jury, and, behind the jury, the public.

The utter simplicity and versatility of the wooden box accounts in part for its durability as an American archetype. It is an easy matter to graft elements of any style onto it, alter its roof pitch and relationship to the street, and thereby produce a "new" image dictated by prevailing taste and native ingenuity. By 1749, a building such as this would have been commonplace, adding its posture to the new pastel-painted and Classical sense of tidiness and order that came to characterize American towns.

The reputed architect of the 1749 Plymouth Courthouse would have been very concerned that the seat of British colonial law convey, within the means available, the presence of British culture, for his sympathies lay squarely with the Tories and the Crown. He was Judge Peter Oliver of Middleborough, and he presided in his own building as Superior Court Justice from 1756 until the Revolution, when he left Boston with the British army for England, where he died in 1791. He supported the incorporation of British courtroom decorum—wigs, robes, and ceremony—into the practice of American jurisprudence, and even took to riding his circuit in the majesty of a coach-and-four emblazoned with his arms and attended by postilions and scarlet-clad outriders, to be met and escorted to the courthouse by town officials and citizens of note.

Beginning around 1680, Boston's merchants started transforming the town from wood to brick. Their twin desires to avoid a repetition of several disastrous fires and to become more culturally aligned with their English counterparts were requited by a sudden influx of artisans and craftsmen from urban Britain who became New England's first corps of trained builders. They imported knowledge of mercantile middle-class English architecture and it spread rapidly through New England. This new architecture was a fusion of English Renaissance Classicism and stylistic elements which the British had borrowed from the Netherlands—building in brick with prominent double-pitched (gambrel) roofs, regular rows of dormers, double-hung windows, balustrades, and narrow glazed cupolas atop buildings of greater pretension. They imported at the same time the predominant Netherlandish housing type of post-fire London, the simple two- or three-story brick rowhouse separated from the next house by a continuous firewall that extended above the roof. This solid brick end-wall became popular even for freestanding houses, and was the excuse for imaginative architectural treatments—sundials, sculpted chimneys, statuary, and stepped gable tops. Most of the prominent merchants of Boston and other mercantile centers built such houses for themselves. They were monumental and grand, as befitted their social preeminence. And when they turned to the erection of public buildings and faced the dilemma of creating an appropriate architectural image for their sacred and secular institutions, they simply resorted to making enlarged versions of their own suitably grand houses. The substantive quality that separates the MacPhaedris-Warner House (1716) in Portsmouth, New Hampshire (fig. 1), from Massachusetts Hall at Harvard (1718) or from Boston's Old State House (1712) is principally a matter of size. These buildings are no more than elongated houses. Monuments were then made from domestic architecture by enlarging them and adding a cupola.

1 The MacPhaedris-Warner House (1716), Portsmouth, New Hampshire (John McConnell)

In May 1712, Samuel Sewall, early Boston diarist and later Chief Justice of the Superior Court of Judicature, lay the cornerstone (after having carved his initials in it) of a new building to house the provincial legislature, the royal governor and his cabinet, town government, the Superior Court of Judicature, and the inferior Court of Common Pleas of Suffolk County. Built and perhaps designed by a William Payne on the site of the wooden Town House destroyed by fire in 1711, this was the first Old State House. When this new building also burned in December 1747, the brick walls that remained standing were incorporated into a reconstruction the following year, and it is this Old State House that stands today (pl. 61). The building was not substantively changed from its 1712 appearance: it retained the same dimensions (36 by 112 feet), brick walls, basement, two stories, and an attic punctuated by dormers, as well as the ornate Flemish stepped endwalls. But the carved scrolls atop the gables gave way to symbols of empire: the lion and unicorn. Other changes dictated by taste were made. The original Dutch gambrel roof became a simple pitched roof, shorn of its balustrade, and the octagonal cupola was rebuilt as the slender three-stage lantern we know today.

During the period of its greatest role in American political history, the Old State House did not appear as the chaste brick reconstruction that currently stands at the head of State Street. In 1773, in accord with established American acceptance of ersatz construction, the whole exterior was painted to resemble masonry with a stone-colored paint to which sand was added for stonelike texture. (The New State House, which Charles Bulfinch designed as a replacement for the Old, was similarly treated.) The history of the Old State House is well documented, and our age might be astounded at the variety of guises, some drastic and some bizarre, that has disfigured the building through more than two and one-half centuries of use as a courthouse, state house, and city hall; as shops, offices, manufactories, and museums. Such was the state of degradation in 1876, the very year the nation celebrated its centennial, that it was almost demolished as a traffic impediment. The city fathers were humiliated into its preservation only by a bid from Chicago to purchase, dismantle, and re-erect it on the shores of Lake Michigan.

The courts met in the court chamber at the west (uphill) end of the second floor, and continued in this location until, after the Revolution, they removed to the "new" courthouse in School Street, designed by Thomas Dawes. This building was replaced in 1810 by Charles Bulfinch's Suffolk Courthouse, the nation's first granite building, which was itself demolished for the construction of Old City Hall on the same site in 1861.

After the Revolution

Boston was the child of my father
and he did pretty much as he pleased
with it.
—FRANCIS VAUGHAN BULFINCH

If one has the impression from the preceding discussion that Charles Bulfinch had some significant role in the architecture of postrevolutionary New England, this is because, more than any other single man, Bulfinch was responsible for transforming Boston from a provincial and largely medieval town, ransacked by the British, into a cosmopolitan and progressive city, adorned with scores of architectural jewels that were the very picture of urbanity in the English-speaking world. And it was precisely this English world that remained for New Englanders the object of attention and source of wealth long after the political break of 1776.

There was no cultural break in New England to parallel the revolution in government. The wealthy merchants and civic leaders of Newport, Boston, Salem, Newburyport, and Portsmouth continued to rely chiefly on trade with Britain for their wealth, and when they invested that wealth in buildings for themselves and their community, they built pictures of their cultural conservatism. As a class, they came from Puritan stock and took as their social peers their middle-class counterparts in Britain. The architecture that they preferred was correspondingly a chaste and understated version of contemporary British work. The models generally employed were all from the architectural work of the Scot Robert Adam, who as a young man had gone on the Grand Tour, visited Rome and Pompeii, and was influenced by the exquisitely delicate mosaics and frescoes of Roman interiors. This decorative finesse he reworked into a modern idiom of decorated Classical forms which he applied to a new spatial approach: rooms of differing shapes and sizes in a single building. His buildings contained round, square, and oval rooms; rooms with vaulted ceilings and rooms with swelling apsidal ends. His columns were often attenuated and pencillike, his decorative forms were finely wrought chains of wheat husks and swags executed in plaster as if they were webs spun by spiders. His exteriors were frequently in brick and exhibit a smooth planar quality into which window openings were cleanly cut.

When the ships' captains and merchants of New England built houses after the war, they did so in the style of Adam, known as the Federal Style. But perhaps as a residue of Puritan taste, which eschewed overt showiness, these homes were even more spare and understated. Possibly the finest remaining example of these Federal Style homes is the several blocks of Chestnut Street in Salem. These rows of houses are simply beautifully proportioned square brick façades, their roofs pitched so shallowly that they are not visible, and their doors set under oval porticoes and crowned with that hallmark of the Federal Style, the graceful oval fanlight.

For Charles Bulfinch the Federal Style was both a point of departure and a sort of stylistic manifesto of taste from which he never deviated. His stylistic uniformity notwithstanding, Bulfinch left one of the most remarkable legacies of a complete architectural worldview ever achieved. His accomplishments include the United States Capitol, three state houses (in Massachusetts, Connecticut, and Maine), twelve churches, six banks, four insurance company buildings, three entire residential streets, and over thirty-two houses, as well as the Boston Latin School, the Massachusetts General Hospital, theaters, prisons, almshouses, hospitals, markets, warehouses, wharves, arches, dormitories, academic buildings, our first urban park (the Boston Common), urban design (the Bulfinch Triangle of streets near North Station where the Mill Pond had been), and, finally, and of special concern here, four courthouses. Two of these (in Boston and Worcester) no longer exist, but the other two (in Cambridge and Newburyport) still do; Newburyport is the oldest Superior Court building still in use as such in the Commonwealth.

Bulfinch was born in Boston of wealthy aristocratic parents in 1763. He was graduated from Harvard College in 1781, whereupon he was sent for a two-year Grand Tour of Europe, as was the custom among the sons of families of consequence. Modern London particularly stunned and fascinated the young man, who had thought of Boston as the height of sophistication. Following his return (after spending time with Thomas Jefferson in France), he resolved to pursue his gentlemanly interest in architecture by speculating in development projects that would remake Boston into a modern cultural capital on the British model. He lost all his money in 1794 through the failure of a development venture building a splendid curving set of rowhouses on both sides of a crescent-shaped park in the middle of what is now Franklin Street. Although the venture forced him into bankruptcy, the Tontine Crescent provided Boston with its first glimpse of monumental town planning and gave America its first professional architect. Bulfinch was forced to take up architecture as a means of supporting himself, thereby beginning the practice of charging clients for architectural services. His charitable fellow citizens, in order to secure his future, elected him chairman of the selectmen and concurrently chief of police, and these two positions, which he held for nearly twenty years, allowed him to pursue his great urban vision with not a small degree of assurance.

In 1805 Bulfinch was engaged in completely rebuilding and enlarging Faneuil Hall. Sensitive to its extraordinary history, he carefully incorporated the earlier Wren/Baroque structure into his enlarged version, keeping the public chambers above the open-arcaded marketplace. When, in that same year, he was called upon to furnish a design for a new courthouse in Newburyport, it is clear that Old Faneuil Hall was very much on his mind. The building he provided, like the Boston landmark, had its principal rooms on the upper story and an open arcade across the front (fig. 2). This two-story brick structure was built on the banks of Frog Pond with its front to the Mall. The center of its roof was adorned with a pedimented gable containing a bull's-eye window and bearing a figure of Justice holding scales in her right hand. Typical of Bulfinch's architecture, the spring-points and keystones of the arches, as well as the stringcourse and window lintels and sills, were of white marble in crisp contrast to the red brick walls.

In 1853, an age characterized by different tastes, the whole building was remodeled in a kind of Italianate mode (pl. 40) with a broad bracketed cornice. The pediment, statue, and arcade were all removed and most of the window openings were given a more stylish, slightly arched, brick lintel. In addition, the front door was monumentalized with a heavy rusticated stone surround capped by a broad segmental pediment. Finally, adding insult to injury, the whole building was coated with mastic cement to resemble stone. This last dressing has been removed, but virtually all that remains of Bulfinch's building is part of the brick endwalls and perhaps the windows facing the pond. Recent renovation has returned some of the simple elegance of the building's original state: graceful door casings (pl. 14)

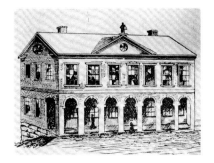

2   The Courthouse and Town House, Newburyport, 1805. Drawing made by Charles M. Hodge (From *The Architecture of Charles Bulfinch* by Harold Kirker [Harvard University Press, 1969])

and window casings with inset shutters, the turned spindle work of both the courtroom furniture and staircase balusters, the pale wall colors, the chandeliers (pl. 39).

Bulfinch's other remaining courthouse in Cambridge was nearly demolished in 1966, but was given a new life in the mid 1980s. It, too, was so substantially altered and enlarged that little of the Bulfinch Building (known by that name) remains on view. When completed in 1816, it was described by the *Columbian Sentinel* as "of brick, remarkably simple, but varied in the form of the windows and arches, and [producing] a pleasing effect from the harmony of its proportions." This evaluation might, indeed, serve well as an apt description of the majority of Bulfinch's work. In 1848 the building was enlarged by architect Ammi B. Young, in total sympathy with the then out-of-fashion Bulfinch style (pl. 49). That the Greek Revivalist Young could add a massive Federal Style cupola and continue Bulfinch's use of blank arcades over the windows is a remarkable example of the proper domination of stylistic unity over personal expression.

In architecture, this age had three giant figures. Bulfinch was one. The second was a man who, if he were only known as an architect, would be highly acclaimed. That he was also a lawyer begins to describe the breadth of his interests. That he was also an inventor, author, naturalist, agriculturalist, educator, ambassador, philosopher, governor of Virginia, and the third president of the United States; that he was all these things and more leads many to see Thomas Jefferson as the most remarkable American ever to exist. If for Bulfinch, Neoclassicism was an approach for adapting the best of modern British architecture to tastefully urbanize America, it was for Jefferson quite the opposite. No anglophile, Jefferson saw in the revival of Classical architecture a potential source for civic architecture that might evince the certainties of civic virtue and blessings of active citizenship in an infant republic that stood to learn much from republican Rome. People needed among them models of Roman architecture to bespeak the duties of republican citizenship—Jefferson's Virginia State Capitol, for example, was a copy of a Roman temple. For Jefferson, architecture possessed a metaphoric correspondence between forms and noble ideals made possible through the associations that history attaches to buildings, and they were useful because of this. His stewardship and practice did much to promote architecture as the most necessary of art forms in a land never fully convinced of the need for art at all.

If it was Jefferson who first profoundly recognized the potential of architecture to generate adequate metaphors by which a new sociopolitical order might understand and reinforce itself, it was Benjamin Henry Latrobe who was first able to see and manifest the more abstract potential of Neoclassicism to embody fundamental and primary forces intrinsic to a nascent American spirit: simplicity, directness, practicality, honesty. Latrobe was born in England in 1764, and he was trained as both an engineer and an architect. When he moved to the United States in 1796 he brought with him training, experience, and talent profoundly in excess of anything known here. In his unfortunately short career he built buildings of extraordinary power and technical excellence. He used Greek rather than Roman forms because they were more primitive and direct, and, working chiefly in stone, he generated a revolutionary new kind of Neoclassicism whose elementary geometric forms appealed, not to the eye or the conscience, but to the intellect. His was a self-revelatory kind of architecture that created order through the rational manner in which his forms explained themselves to the studious observer. His approach to things was transmitted to his chief pupil, Robert Mills, whose customshouses in Newburyport and New Bedford stand in Massachusetts as examples of the unadorned power inherent in monumental simplicity.

Fifty years after the Declaration of Independence, Thomas Jefferson and John Adams were dead. They left behind a nation facing growing sectarian disagreement, which had yet to declare its cultural "Declaration of Independence." By the close of the Revolution there was a growing popular sentiment, at first decidedly anti-British, to be at once free from European cultural domination and to supersede it altogether through a kind of American cultural self-genesis. A token of this feeling was the vote in Congress in 1795, which failed by only two votes, to substitute classical Greek for English as the official language. This same sentiment led to a surprisingly broad popular interest in literature and art, as well as in social and political reform. It led to an architecture, indeed to a culture, of which Charles Bulfinch, ever linked to notions of propriety and tastes formed in his youth, was to remain on the periphery. What came to be was like a new cultural land to which, like Moses, he had led, and into which he was not to enter.

The Greek Revival

The three great staples of New
England are ice and rocks and men.
—CHARLES FRANCIS ADAMS, JR.

Perhaps in part as an effort to sustain the ebullient patriotic sentiments attending our revolutionary victory, which were waning because of growing divisive sectionalism, Americans were emotionally attracted to the cause of the Greek War of Independence from Turkish domination, which began in 1821. This struggle was seen as analogous to our own Revolution, and the sentiment was amplified by the romantic aura surrounding the event, which was propagated in part by Lord Byron's poetic foray into the cause. It served our own national mythos to embrace the reestablishment of democracy on the very soil that had given birth to it.

Europe had already "discovered" ancient Greece, principally under the aegis of her archaeologists. Archaeology had only recently been invented, and the small numbers of men who had unearthed Herculaneum, Spalato, and Pompeii, such as Robert Adam, ranged further afield to ancient Greece. Their activity was only possible because of the "invention" of history as a way of looking at the past during the Enlightenment. For the first time, history was seen to be composed of discrete periods set apart from one another by their own unique constellation of political, social, and cultural forces, and capable of being studied, reconstituted, and analyzed. And used. This sent Europeans out in search of their assumed historical antecedents, first to the Roman world, and subsequently to Greece, mother of their culture and wellspring of noble political constructs.

By following the course of the archaeologists and historians who were delving steadily backward into antiquity, we Americans also arrived at a time felt to be even more analogous to our own situation than that of republican Rome: that of ancient Greece. The Greek polity was understood as simpler and more direct; nobler and truer than Rome. Republican Rome, after all, had rapidly metamorphosed into Imperial Rome with its series of tyrannical despots—hardly an appropriate model for a newly democratic nation.

The touchstone of ancient Greece in 1800, as today, was its buildings and sculpture, which is among any civilization's most enduring legacies. These were just then coming to light and being popularized by the exhibition of the Parthenon's sculptures in Britain by Lord Elgin, and the publication of such monumental works as Stuart and Revett's *The Antiquities of Athens* (London, 1762, et seq.). These first accurate measured drawings of the Parthenon and other temples and monuments dotting the ancient Greek world were stunningly beautiful representations of what Professor William Pierson has called "the supreme visual embodiment of the oldest democracy on earth."

The citizens of Boston in the second decade of the new century began to affect the "Greek manner" in all things: literature, the visual arts, hairstyles, clothing fashions; they even took to naming sons and daughters after the heroes and heroines of Greek mythology. (Thomas Bulfinch, son of the architect, published his *Age of Fable* in Boston in 1855.) That this passion for things Greek coincided with the astounding flowering of accomplishment in Boston earned her the sobriquet "Athens of America." And if she was that, then Harvard College was her Academy. Harvard led the nation's educational institutions by stressing that a broad knowledge of the classics—of Latin and Greek language, drama, philosophy, and scientific literature was the sole avenue by which the well educated might approach life.

It was from this curriculum and the "Greek Mania," as it came to be known, that Boston became an early home of the Greek Revival.

The citizens of New England came to live in Greek houses, worship in Greek churches, shop in Greek markets, and keep money in Greek banks; they frequented learned clubs called Athenaeums, which were intellectual societies for the discussion of the classics and which maintained private art galleries and great libraries. Their shelves were kept filled by the pens of Emerson, Thoreau, Melville, Hawthorne, Longfellow, and the like. This devotion to the mind was simultaneously a devotion to reform; Boston led the nation in advocating free education, expanded suffrage, humane treatment of the insane, temperance, and trade-unionism, to name but a few of the causes. Boston's Mayor Josiah Quincy (1823–1828), later president of Harvard, had its streets cleaned (for the first time in two centuries, some said), built its water and sewage systems, and lectured the Suffolk Grand Jury on prison reform. All the while, from Boston's pulpits and publishing houses came the abolitionist campaign against slavery.

Small wonder, then, that in the intellectual and creative ferment of Boston in the 1820s and 1830s the Greek culture found by archaeologists should fall on such fertile ground half a world and nineteen centuries away. In architecture, too, the devotion to reform and ancient Greece took root and flowered to such an extent that colonial and Federal New England was remade in a new, white, and monumental way. Boston discovered true monumentality in building when it began to build wholesale in granite.

The Greek Revival in Boston has been called "the Granite Style," and it was the marriage of Greek forms with Massachusetts granite that finally and thoroughly accomplished a new way of building and a break with past European styles. Construction in granite doesn't readily allow for the gentility of ornament and subtlety of nuance that characterized earlier forms of architecture. All the powerful simplicity, honesty, and monumental directness of Greek forms on the one hand, and of Americans' estimation of themselves on the other, received for the first time its consummate expression in the granite public buildings put up first in Massachusetts, and then all along the eastern and gulf coasts with granite from Massachusetts quarries.

It is not, then, surprising that Solomon Willard, quixotic and multifaceted entrepreneur of the first great granite quarries in Quincy, should also turn out to be the architect of the first Greek granite Superior Courthouse building in the Commonwealth. Willard (1783–1861) was the son of a Pembroke carpenter and cabinetmaker, and he came to Boston, at age twenty, skilled in his father's trades. Essentially self taught, he mastered woodcarving, stonecutting, sculpture, architecture, quarrying, and, finally, scientific farming in his sixty-eight years. He is credited with the design of ducted hot-air central heating, with the development of the Quincy granite quarries, and with the singlehanded invention of all the tools used in handling and transporting massive stone blocks. He carved the fenceposts at the Old Granary Burying Ground, as well as the figureheads for scores of Boston's clipper ships. But he is chiefly remembered as the architect of such works as the Bunker Hill Monument, the Quincy Town Hall, and the new Superior Courthouses for Suffolk and Norfolk counties, all built in granite.

The Suffolk County Courthouse in Boston (fig. 3) no longer stands, but it occupied a site on Court Street where the School Committee Building now stands. Noted mostly for its severity, it was described upon completion in 1836 as "a granite barn with a porch at either end." It nevertheless made an unambiguous statement about the directness and monumentality of justice in Suffolk County, which was a reiteration of a theme Willard also had made in 1827 in Dedham with his Norfolk County Courthouse, which happily still stands. Though altered several times, the building retains something of its Greek Revival character (pl. 41).

3 Old Suffolk Courthouse, Boston (Courtesy of The Bostonian Society and Boston Redevelopment Authority)

Willard's building in Dedham replaced a 1796 wooden structure (which had had a cupola by Bulfinch and a bell by Paul Revere) in order to fulfill the Court of General Sessions' desire "to take into consideration, among other things, the subject of erecting a fireproof building for the safe-keeping of records." Willard was commissioned and the contractors Damon & Bates were hired to construct a building "in the form of an ancient Greek temple with columns at both ends." At a final cost of $30,000, the building was dedicated on July 4, 1825, with appropriate Masonic ceremonies and a cornerstone containing, among other things, a silver plate with the names of John Quincy Adams, president of the United States, and Levi Lincoln, governor of the Commonwealth; specimens of Dedham-made marbleized paper; and a small beaver hat of local manufacture.

Sounding a cry that was to become an old saw to those who inhabit and administer courthouses, the commissioners recognized in 1860 that the courthouse needed more space, and determined to have it, against vociferous local opposition, by extending Willard's building rather than by constructing a new building across the street. The courthouse was thus enlarged according to the plans of prominent Boston architect Gridley J. Fox Bryant (designer of Old City Hall, among numerous other landmarks). Bryant extended the north front, sensitively retaining Willard's Doric portico, which today is the only visible remnant of the original building. He also added flanking wings to the east and west. Less sensitively, Bryant added a grandiose and totally incongruous dome to the whole composition (domes are strictly Roman and alien to Greek architecture), the whole thing done at the then-scandalous cost of $75,000. Bryant designed in a time whose spirit was far different from the naive optimism of the 1820s; his world was one desperately anxious to reaffirm prevailing institutions in the face of the fratricidal hatreds and institutional underminings of the Civil War.

In 1890 the county hired Wait & Cutter, architects of Boston, and proceeded with a third major reconstitution of the building, this time adding a major wing to the rear and renovating inside and out (pls. 42, 43, 44), replacing the old dome with an even more grandiose one. It is this building, standing today, which was the location of much of the courtroom proceedings in the 1921–27 trial of Sacco and Vanzetti. With the exception of the dome, the present building exhibits a remarkable degree of stylistic integrity, owing to the willingness of later architects to subsume their personal tastes to those of Solomon Willard, building both in his style and his material.

New Bedford also built a Greek temple to house its Superior Court after it was made a half shiretown of Bristol County in 1828. New Bedford typifies towns whose first major period of growth occurred after the turn of the nineteenth century (like Worcester or Nantucket) during the heyday of the Greek Revival. In New Bedford, the courthouse (fig. 4) was designed by Russell Warren (1783–1860) from Rhode Island, who worked extensively in New Bedford and was the principal Greek Revivalist in his home state (with James C. Bucklin he designed the Providence Arcade of 1828). The courthouse is simply one of many noteworthy Greek structures in the historic center of town—the Customs House by Robert Mills, the Fishermen's Exchange, and the Old City Hall (now part of the public library) also by Warren are but a few. The 1831 Superior Courthouse differs from Willard's in its use of a somewhat more decorative Ionic order, its wooden columns topped by double-scrolled capitals (Willard used the Doric order). It embodies the graceful good proportions of that order as advanced by a multitude of architects' and builders' pattern books published in this era, which contained detailed drawings for the accurate construction of all the Greek orders. (*The American Builder's Companion,* 1827, by Boston architect Asher Benjamin was one of the most popular.) Among the standards of fame for early courthouses appears to be whether or not Daniel Webster ever tried a case therein. The famous orator pleaded a case in this New Bedford Superior Courthouse in 1835, which was considered an event important enough to close all the public schools for the day to allow teachers and pupils alike to hear him.

And yet this was not the event that made the building well known, but rather the trial fifty years later of Lizzie Borden for the murder of her parents with an axe. Behind the original building, where architect Nat C. Smith's 1899 addition is now, there were stables for visiting attorneys to use. During the weeks of this sensational trial they were outfitted as telegraph stations from which members of the fourth estate filed national dispatches on the conduct of the members of the third.

4   New Bedford Courthouse, Bristol County (Keller & Peet Associates)

The design serves well to recall a major drawback to the indiscriminate use of the Greek temple for all sorts of building types, a situation that had rapidly evolved. Judging from the evidence, it was frequently felt that in its pure form the Greek temple was somehow not satisfyingly monumental enough, and the old prerevolutionary practice of adorning important buildings with cupolas and belfries was continued. The addition of such architectural doodads generally pleased traditionalists and horrified purists. Ammi B. Young's Boston Customs House of 1837 was much maligned for marrying a Roman dome to a Greek temple, but most Greek Revival churches continued to carry steeples as their predecessors had. The cupola atop the New Bedford Courthouse today seems considerably more integrated with its setting than does the 1953 Probate Court addition to the building, which is a modern version of old Georgian architecture.

The original courthouse at Barnstable (fig. 5) shares with that at New Bedford many things: it, too, has a belfry crowning its temple front, it carries a number of later additions, and its massive columns are made of wood. And it, too, could boast of the one-time presence of Daniel Webster. But, unlike New Bedford, the Barnstable Courthouse is built of solid rough-faced Quincy granite with pilasters at the corners of dressed granite. And, squarely in the American tradition of materials masquerading as other materials, what appear to be four monolithic granite Doric columns carrying their correctly detailed Doric entablature are actually made of wood that has been painted with sanded paint to resemble stone. The use of granite and the severity of style lend credence to the generally accepted attribution of the design to Boston's leading Greek Revival architect, Alexander Parris (1780–1852). Born in Hebron, Maine, Parris had been a schoolteacher in Pembroke and was trained as a carpenter. When he came to Boston, he became part of a group of young men gathered around Charles Bulfinch, and he served as Bulfinch's superintendent of construction for his great granite Massachusetts General Hospital (1818–23) while Bulfinch was in Washington supervising completion of the Capitol. Parris's own masterpieces in Boston include the Sears House (now the Somerset Club) on Beacon Street (1816), St. Paul's Cathedral on Tremont Street (1819) for which Solomon Willard carved the Ionic capitals, and his masterwork of 1825, the Quincy Market—all Greek and all granite.

The imposing severity of the Barnstable Courthouse is in sharp contrast to both the elegant tall Greek front door and the surprisingly delicate courtroom (pl. 19), which is perhaps the most beautiful in the Commonwealth. The judge's bench sits behind a row of graceful balusters and in front of a screen of Ionic columns and pilasters. The room is surrounded by a lyrical frieze of Greek anthemion palmettes and topped with a gently swelling arched ceiling from which vantage point a Sacred Cod looks down.

Expansions carried out in 1879, 1893, and 1906 (by Guy Lowell,

5   Barnstable Courthouse, Barnstable County

designer of the Boston Museum of Fine Arts) greatly enlarged the structure without seriously compromising its original architectural integrity. Once again, architectural sensitivity dictated all work to be done consonant with the original. Subsequent additions in 1925 and 1972 are less happy—blond brick appendages with steel sash windows, fortunately relegated to the rear of the complex. Through a century and a half of alteration, the image of the chaste temple in splendid isolation amid a green and benign landscape was never molested, and it stands today as the quintessence of the Greek Revival in New England (pl. 20).

Ammi Burnham Young (1798–1874) has already been encountered as the architect who enlarged Bulfinch's Cambridge Courthouse. A pupil of Alexander Parris, Young was a prolific architect in his own right and designed two of our courthouses besides Cambridge. He was born in Lebanon, New Hampshire, and by age thirty-nine he was at the forefront of the Greek Revival with his State Capitol at Montpelier, Vermont (1837) and his popular Boston Customs House (1837–47) with which he achieved an echo of the structural truth of Greek temples (colonnades on all sides and not just the front), thus transcending the merely scenographic act of applying a temple front to an ordinary building. His Worcester Courthouse is Greek; his Lowell Courthouse is not, and is discussed later. Still relatively young at the height of the Greek Revival, Young's architecture changed with the times, and when the Greek mania passed, he proved himself equally adroit at other styles.

For the principal façade of his Worcester Courthouse (1843), he chose the ornate Corinthian order, with fluted columns and a cluster of sprouting leaves for a capital. There were only two of these in the original building (Corinthian columns are the most expensive to carve!), and they were placed according to Greek custom *in antis*, within a porch created in the front bearing wall. This custom derives from the *megaron*, an archaic Greek house type. As was typical, he placed the principal chambers on the upper story, and, perhaps because he was stung by academic criticism of his Customs House, he elected to keep the lovely dome covering the courtrooms invisible from the exterior, hidden below the low Grecian roofline. This ribbed half-dome (pl. 23), which so ennobles the courtroom, is carried on a semicircle of freestanding Ionic columns, making the judges' bench the focus of the entire space.

Young's Quincy granite building is now the left-hand pavilion of a much larger complex (pl. 21) but, except for the slightly darker patina of age, is not obvious as having been a separate structure. By the time the building was enlarged in 1898, Classical Greek architecture was once more in fashion (pl. 10) after fifty years in decline, so that the addition blends perfectly with the original.

Salem is quite unique in the architectural richness of its courthouse complex, which is by itself a good short course in American architectural history. Its courthouses of 1636, 1679 (scene of the witchcraft trials), 1718 (home of the provincial legislature in exile from Boston prior to the Revolution), and 1785 are no longer standing, but those of 1841, 1861, 1889, 1909, and 1981 are. The earliest of this group, queued up along Federal Street (fig. 10), is a Greek Revival structure, virtually indistinguishable in most major regards from Young's Worcester Courthouse. It too is of granite with twin Corinthian columns *in antis*, and it was completed two years earlier than the one in Worcester. It was designed by Richard Bond (1797–1861) of Boston, an architect of some local repute whose Gore Hall Library at Harvard (1838) was as flamboyantly Gothic as his Salem Courthouse was Greek. None of the 1841 interiors remain, and the building now houses the civil division of the court.

Having been championed in New England, the Greek Revival moved on. It spread first to other metropolitan centers of the East and to rural New England, where it was disseminated mostly through the ever-popular builder's guides which accompanied settlers everywhere they went beyond the pale of the architectural profession. The "national style" gave to New England folk villages the appearance of the nest of cozy white homes and red barns popularized by Currier and Ives and actually created by carpenters designing with their planes and saws an inventive wood version of citified high-style Greek work. The Greek Revival even became as simple as building a house with its gable end to the street in imitation of a pediment, and applying white paint. In towns of some means the erection of a public building might still call for a material more durable than wood, as it did in 1858 in Edgartown when Dukes County built its courthouse. About it little is known. Its architect was Harold Sleeper, and its style is carpenter Greek. It sits snugly on Main Street (fig. 6) amidst lush foliage (one of its towering pair of elms was lost a few years ago), and is less monumental than the Greek Revival Methodist Church next door. Edgartown even today is still predominantly a Greek Revival town, which makes it all the more odd that the courthouse is stylistically more conservative than its neighbors. Its brick walls with simple stone lintels at the windows, its simple cubic shape, flat roof, and Classical entrance portico make it reminiscent of fifty-year-old Federal Style architecture. But it is wrapped in a heavy wooden Greek cornice and entablature supported across the front by four flat pilaster strips intended to appear as columns. The large courtroom on the second floor (pl. 45) is as chaste and elegant as the exterior, with its full cornice and entablature, coffer molding and ceiling rosette all done in molded plaster. The building exemplifies the beauty possible from even naively done Greek work.

The Greek Revival crossed the Appalachians with pioneers, some of whom packed builder's pattern books in their wagons and saddlebags. It went further west where the first log cabins were replaced within a decade by astonishingly civilized Greek houses,

6   Edgartown Courthouse, Dukes County (Keller & Peet Associates)

churches, schools, and courthouses. It was almost literally the very vessel used to transmit American culture, through her institutions, to the furthest edge of her frontier.

Apart from the natural desire for stylistic change, the end of the Greek Revival in the North was brought about in part by its acceptance in the South. Southern "Greek Apologists" like Calhoun claimed legitimacy for the institution of human bondage by trumpeting the fact that the ancient democratic Greek city-states had been a slaveholding society. Made thus distasteful and passé in the North, the Greek Revival remained popular in the South. There were few towns in the South, and the style was applied wholesale to the plantation manor houses being built in the "New South"—the states of Alabama, Mississippi, and Louisiana. These states were only then being cultivated by planters from the Old South along the seaboard, who moved swiftly west as their soil was depleted by the practice of raising huge amounts of a single crop. These plantation homes, set behind verandahs nestled in a screen of enormous white columns at the end of a mile-long driveway, were, together with buildings in the distant West, the last of the Greek Revival with its promise of a simple egalitarian democracy in an idealistic land. This was plainly counter to experience; the Greek Revival ends with sectional conflict, loss of faith. The white temple sailed away west on the grassy sea or faded into a humid dream amidst the Spanish moss.

Romanticism

The pleasure of the senses I can sympathize with and share, but the substitution of sensuous ecstasy for intellectual activity is the very devil.
—GEORGE BERNARD SHAW

By the 1850s buildings in different regions of the nation were saying entirely different things with the same language, Greek Classicism. This disparity within our national style was symptomatic of a far deeper schism opening up in the federal union. We had become, at least culturally, three nations: the raw and restless West; the conservative agricultural South tied to an economic system of a subjugated work force, a single crop, and rapid land exhaustion; and the progressive North, rapidly becoming urban and industrial. The litany of events and issues that led to our Civil War is well known. Their cultural effects are less so, and yet they changed our national character no less profoundly than the war did.

Eli Whitney perhaps influenced the course of American history as deeply as any lawgiver, architect, writer, or revolutionary. He is both the inventor of the cotton gin (1794) and the father of mass production through standardized parts. The former invention simultaneously reduced drastically the cost of cotton and exponentially boosted demand for textiles made from it. The resultant wholesale dedication to cotton production in the South and explosive development of the textile industry in the North brought about the polarization of American society. In the North, especially, the change was enormous. Early industry in Rhode Island and Massachusetts, beginning in 1793 with Slater's Mill in Pawtucket, was water-powered and therefore clean, quiet, and limited in scale. Subsequent experiments by such men as Francis Cabot Lowell and Kirk Boott in Waltham, Lowell, Lawrence, and other places established the possibility of manufacture based on utopian industrial communities in which the company provided good housing, education, and even religious opportunity for its workers. They were successful for a time and seemed to promise both commercial viability and social rectitude integrated with a vision of tranquil and domesticated nature. Too much success, perhaps, plus the rise of a mill-owning elite and the supplanting of water power by steam transformed industry from benign and exemplary to exploitive, polluting, and as huge as it was profitable. In the political arena this engendered corruption; in the social, it caused glaring class division between rich and poor. It wrought a kind of spiritual surrender to economic "necessity," the failure of utopian experiment, the burgeoning of both cities and their squalor, and, finally, the despoiling of nature.

As a people, we experienced, like orphaned adolescents, a virtual "end of innocence." By 1850 our cultural and political leaders had not known the Revolution, and what had seemed our national optimism and sense of purpose were compromised as issues of economy and livelihood formed the great shear plane along which the forces holding us together came undone. The sense of loss was profound. The conditions of northern cities and southern plantations alike put the lie to Jefferson's treasured hope for a secure Arcadian nation of farmers which would be at one with the splendid beauty and fecundity of the American land. We looked *back* for the first time in a new way— wistfully, with less confidence in ourselves, wishing things to be as simple and clear as they had seemed in the past.

The white temple took on new meaning: no longer useful for its metaphoric political value or the intellectual appeal of its abstraction, it had one more lesson to teach. This was visual appeal: appeal to emotion rather than reason, through visual stimulation, which is a defining characteristic of the broad cultural movement known as Romanticism. The discovery that architecture had the power to evoke distant times or places—times of immense appeal because of their mystery or self-assuredness—led to a new emotional way of making and thinking about buildings which was abetted by unparalleled technological prowess for manufacturing new building materials (terra cotta, cast iron, and plate glass, for example). As a consequence, the forms of architecture sought after were those that could make evocations of bygone times and exotic places appropriate to the new and multifarious ways we wished to see ourselves.

The development of this polymorphous and democratic culture demanded of architecture more diversity than the Classical tradition was capable of giving. The architecture of markedly *preindustrial* ages, such as medieval Europe or Renaissance Tuscany, was preferred, and qualities antithetical to the Greek Revival came to dominate: irregularity rather than symmetry, rough surfaces rather than smooth, and color and randomness rather than whiteness and order. Architecture was now needed which could provide a sort of fantasy to prop up our sagging ideals. One now might live in an Italianate house, worship in a Gothic church, shop in a Moorish department store, keep money in a Romanesque bank, stop by one's Renaissance club before an evening in a Byzantine theater, and, finally, pass to the Great Reward through Egyptian cemetery gates. Buildings became pictures, frequently wedded to a complementary landscape, of their inhabitants' fantasies, and this ushered in a period of revivals of styles prized for their associational attributes and capacity to give visual delight through those characteristics—roughness, color, the impression of spontaneity, asymmetry—which, when taken together, formed a sort of unwritten code known as the Picturesque.

The two basic Picturesque architectural modes during the Romantic period, which lasted in this country from around 1840 until the 1890s, were derived from the two great traditions in architecture: the Gothic and the Classical. The Gothic Revival was initially an ecclesiastical movement, concentrating its efforts on churches in accord with correct liturgical practice. But the sheer beauty of Gothic forms, quite apart from their organic structural clarity or association with proper Christianity, soon made them popular for all sorts of buildings from houses to hospitals. And the Classical tradition continued unabated from the Greek Revival, but now looked to less ancient models, such as Renaissance Italy and Germany, or Romanesque or Baroque France. If builders were somewhat more interested in correct taste through associational exemplar than in romantic picturesqueness, they generally built in various Renaissance Revival modes.

In the decades following the Civil War, these remained the two predominant architectural categories, but they changed along with the country following that fratricidal nightmare. It was as if our ability to believe in the transcendence and goodness of humankind had passed with the end of the war. That, together with all the grimness of the unchecked barbarousness of our industrial system, the economic depression of 1872, and the blatant corruption of Grant's administration in Washington and of government in general, led to a nation that put its faith in the tangible, the durable, and the obvious. Chief among possessions are buildings. In periods of increased devotion to things material, architecture tends to become more ornate and self-important. Classicism became dominated by the French Second Empire Baroque, with its protruding and receding wall planes, swelling mansard roofs, layers upon layers of expressed floors, and its profusion of ornament in the form of doubled and tripled bunches of columns and sculpted human and vegetable forms. Boston's Old City Hall is an understated example.

On the Gothic side, architecture was heavily influenced by the teaching of England's avatar of taste, John Ruskin. While maintaining the inherent righteousness of Gothic architecture, he was predominantly interested in the ornamental possibilities of it, particularly of a local example found in Venice and northern Italy. Venetian, or Ruskinian Gothic, architecture, so embraced by Victorian England, was characterized by bristling, exaggerated silhouettes and *constructional polychromy,* which is the use of naturally colored materials side-by-side for the purely visual delight of their colors. This was a style in which ornament and pattern predominated in accord with the Victorian *horror vaccui,* making the unadorned surface a positive rarity. English and American cities, blackened by an industrial pall, accepted these vigorously colored and articulated buildings as an antidote. Some of the very best remaining examples of Ruskinian Gothic buildings in the country are in Massachusetts: Memorial Hall at Harvard, the Pittsfield Athenaeum, and the new Old South Church at Copley Square in Boston.

Throughout the United States, designers of courthouses generally eschewed Gothic styles, and Massachusetts possesses one of the very few (at Fitchburg). All the rest of the courthouses from this period derive from romantic variants of Classicism, because for most of our history there has been an ineluctable bond between government buildings and Classical architecture. The earliest of these favored styles in Massachusetts was the Bracketed, or "Italianate," derived from the farmhouses of Tuscany and the Italian Campagna and characterized by asymmetry, towers, roundheaded windows (frequently grouped in pairs), and broadly overhanging cornices supported on florid carved brackets. This approach proved more suited to Picturesque Romantic tastes partially because, unlike the Greek Revival, it was more flexible by having no fixed vocabulary of formal pieces and no canonic set of rules governing proper usage and proportion.

Plymouth County turned its 1749 building over to the Town of Plymouth and built itself a new courthouse in 1820. Its contract with a local designer/builder, John Bates, produced a building at the dawn of the Greek Revival already at least a half century out of style (fig. 7). It was this late-Georgian Palladian building (Daniel Webster appeared here, too!), so characteristic of American coastal architecture in the last quarter century before the Revolution, that was incorporated into an expansion and renovation in 1857, also done by Bates (who called himself an architect by then) and built by mason Edmund

7 Plymouth Courthouse (1820) (Courtesy of The Pilgrim Society, Plymouth, Mass.)

Robbins of Plymouth. The 1820 building was expanded by two bays on each end. The central on-axis entryway, its centrality reinforced by the pediment-crowned bay, was eliminated and awkwardly replaced by the ambiguity of twin entrances to either side. Stylistic elements of the earlier building were repeated—cornice, Corinthian pilasters, quion blocks at the corners—and, in fact, Georgian elements were added—the balustrade above the cornice, the glazed cupola in place of the old belfry. These were married to purely Greek entry porticoes and some more-or-less Italianate hood moldings, bracketed sills at the roundheaded windows (pl. 79), and the flared gable under which Justice in her niche remained. The whole was then painted chocolate brown to resemble then-fashionable brownstone. The cupola and part of the roof burned in 1881, and when it was rebuilt, the cupola appeared as a stretched-out version of the original.

Today the building stands, with additions from 1881 and 1962, as our most architecturally curious courthouse. Its charming appearance has been compromised by the gradual alteration of its elm trees, plantings, and balustraded square in favor of a bituminous parking lot —an object lesson in the importance of proper landscape design for the spaces that must inevitably accompany monumental buildings.

The egregiously unkempt and compromised landscape surrounding the grandiose courthouse at Lowell does not invite a visitor to go around to the back of the complex to see the original courthouse built in 1850 by Ammi B. Young, who by then was working in non-Greek Revival styles. It is this mostly Romanesque building (fig. 8) which of all the Superior Court buildings is most closely associated with Daniel Webster. In 1897 it was moved back from Gorham Street and masked by a new imposing structure to which it was appended. Rectangular in plan, with pavilions at either end, it cost $100,000 and was made of bright red brick with white painted decoration that, surprisingly, was made completely of cast iron. All of its heavy round window hoods, their supporting colonnettes, arch bands, and inserted panels of diamond diaperwork are made of cast iron; so is the cupola with its clock faces and bright blue top. This cupola still carries the Scales of Justice that peek over the top of the main building. The "Daniel Webster Courtroom" (pls. 9, 69) occupies the central portion of the upper story. The outer walls of this upper story terminate, not in a bracketed Italianate cornice, but rather in both horizontal and raking machicolations, a band of toothlike corbeled arches derived from defensive features of medieval architecture.

The Lawrence Courthouse of 1858 and that of Salem of 1861 were both originally Italianate structures, and both are changed. Lawrence placed its new courthouse beside Ammi B. Young's 1849 city hall, the two buildings facing the common. The building has a broadly overhanging cornice and cupola, and was designed by city engineer James K. Barber so that its main entry and principal façade were on Common Street. Situated thus, it sat in its own small landscaped

8   Old Lowell Courthouse, Middlesex County (Charles Cowley, *History of Lowell* [Boston: Lee & Shepard; Lowell: B. C. Sargeant and Joshua Merrill, 1868])

park. Only two years after its completion, it burned and was rebuilt immediately. Subsequent renovation in 1900 so altered the building that, as it stands today, it belongs to another era and will be discussed later.

A similar fate befell Salem's 1861 courthouse, built by architect Enoch Fuller and contractors Simeon Flint and Abraham Towle immediately beside the 1841 courthouse. Though stylistically altered in 1889 (this alteration will be discussed later), enough of its interior remains intact to give a sense of its original style. It was a simple two-story block whose Federal Street façade was divided horizontally and vertically into thirds. It had three bays, the center of which was brought slightly forward and crowned by a pedimented dormer. Horizontally it was divided into base, principal upper story with corner quoins and a great cornice, and a visible hipped roof crowned with a balustrade, so that, on the whole, it resembled the villas of wealthy Renaissance Italians. It had, furthermore, very Italianate windows (pl. 5)—two rounded panes gathered into one roundheaded opening with a circular light of colored glass, all topped by heavy hooded moldings. These still grace the remaining old courtroom.

Finally, it should be recalled that Bulfinch's courthouse at Newburyport was "brought up to date" in 1853, and its hooded windows and bracketed cornice typify what was thought of as Italianate architecture.

Associating the administration of the law with Gothic architecture seems to have been difficult for the midcentury mind. The Gothic had always had its most credible associations with areas of faith and religion—it was, after all, an architectural system developed by the great cathedral builders of the Middle Ages. Nevertheless, in some cases the Romantic mind succeeded in divorcing both the abstract sublimity and the visual delight of its forms from its ecclesiastical connotations. That done, those emotions could be applied to other institutions. The law, however, was a fairly discriminating Classical Club, and Gothic was seldom admitted.

It is, then, something of a surprise to find a Gothic courthouse. But in 1869, when the Fitchburg Courthouse (pl. 35) was built, the Gothic was becoming the architectural style par excellence in Victorian America. Plans were secured from E. Boyden & Sons of Worcester, and the building took its place on the town square alongside the public library, armory, and the similarly Gothic Christ Church. The building was greater than eighty feet square and its walls were laid up in rock-faced granite that had been quarried locally and hauled to the site by oxen. In a smooth-faced state, the same material is used for the trim work set in these walls, which are laid with characteristically beaded joints in reddish colored mortar. The courthouse cost $125,000.

The building teaches us that the Gothic is as vertical a style as the Classical is horizontal, and to that one can ascribe its associations with upward motion and dynamic aspiration. Gothic windows are tall and narrow (pl. 36); thin pointed dormers and iron crestings integrate the building with the sky, and the roofs are steeply pitched. A sense of the dynamism inherent in Victorian Gothic architecture is carried from the massing to the smallest detail—columns at the entryway arch appear as active pistons pushing upward against their load. Analogies between architectural and machine parts are apt in this case, because this was an age characterized by the apotheosis of the machine, which had come to produce much of the articles used in daily life, from teaspoons to building parts.

For whatever reason, the bold and assuredly Gothic promise of the building is not fulfilled on the interior as successfully as the exterior. Here the use of Gothic forms is more tentative and thin, and the typically Ruskinian love of decorated surfaces is not in evidence, except in the golden oak furnishings and the Gothic dado in the courtroom (pls. 7, 37, 38). The replacement of the original pointed windows with standard rectangular ones is unfortunate. That the glory of this building is its exterior, however, is not atypical of Victorian buildings in general, for this was an object-fixated age. So much concern was spent in elaborating the scenographic exterior of a building that often little thought was expended on its innards.

Happily, this building continues to sit in a well-tended parklike setting. Thus situated, the building is fused with its landscape, and the interdependence so valued by the Romantic mind is therefore retained.

There are parallels to be made between the 1861 Salem Courthouse, described above, and the 1871 Berkshire County Courthouse in Pittsfield (pl. 66), and yet, although they are separated by only a decade, they are pronouncedly different in style and character. In Pittsfield we encounter for the first time a building appearing to be two decades ahead of its time. It is true that some of its details belie its age, but its architect, Louis Weisbein of Boston, conceived of it with such academically correct Classical proportions that it anticipates the much later infatuation with monumental Classicism.

Nevertheless, it is a Renaissance Revival building, and still within the Romantic movement. Its basis is the work of a leading Renaissance Italian architect, Andrea Palladio (1508–1580), whose churches, urban palazzi, and countryside villas probably form the most influential and imitated corpus of buildings in the history of architecture. The deification of Palladio by subsequent generations was in part the result of the repeated publication of his *Four Books on Architecture*, an extended treatise on both theory and practical matters illustrated with his own works. His influence was strongly felt in England and her colonies, and colonial Americans built Palladian buildings after 1750 or so. The 1820 Plymouth Courthouse is a good example (fig. 7). Thomas Jefferson was among the first Americans to possess a copy of Palladio's book, and both he and Bulfinch drew heavily on it for designs.

The customary architectural formulas derived from Palladio's villas stressed a vertical division of the façade into a tripartite A-B-A rhythm, with the central B part generally set forward and crowned with a pediment. Furthermore, there was a horizontal division into thirds: a base story, usually rusticated masonry (deeply recessed joints) or an arcade; the main floors above gathered into one statement, usually accompanied by columns or pilasters of the colossal order (more than a single story); and a cap formed by a Classical cornice and low hipped roof.

Pittsfield originally had a short mansard roof with roundheaded dormers, a Second Empire element that made the building appear more of its age. This was replaced at the turn of the century with a more Classical parapet wall, thereby relieving the building of its only rather residential element. Otherwise, it is built according to Palladian precepts. Weisbein may have encountered Palladio through the school of architecture at M.I.T., which was the nation's first, having been started in 1865. Although the building also reflects the substantial Beaux-Arts French over-elaboration taught at M.I.T., Weisbein may have used Palladio's Villa Pisani, outside Padua, as a model. A flight of monumental stairs leads to a recessed entry porch set in the rusticated Sheffield light blue marble ground story, which is surmounted by a grand main and third floors treated as one story in smoothly dressed white marble with colossal order pilasters and a Corinthian temple front in the central bay. Only the pairs of segmental arched windows in the ground story and the brackets supporting the cornice are obvious elements of an earlier architectural vocabulary.

The courthouse was built by A. B. and D. C. Munyan of Pittsfield for a cost of $200,000. Its erection was the result of a protracted struggle that lasted from 1812 until 1868, between forces divided on whether to move the county seat from Lenox to Pittsfield. An enactment of the General Court was finally promulgated on June 8, 1868, and construction started on October 26, demonstrating the speed at which architects move when they have to.

On the other hand, the speed at which building committees usually move can be demonstrated by the fact that it took almost a decade for the construction of the Suffolk County Courthouse in Boston (1886–1895). Even without its 1938 office tower, it is by far the largest of our courthouses, and the last still within the Romantic tradition. It is Classical—officially German Renaissance—and to some romantic classicism would seem a contradiction in terms. But it must be remembered that Classicism in these instances was still used more for emotional associations evoked in viewers than for more purely intellectual reasons, and it is this appeal to emotion that distinguishes the

Romantic sensibility in architecture, music, literature, and other forms of art, from other eras.

The design was supposed to be the result of a two-stage competition, but there was much grumbling when the second stage was cancelled and the commission awarded to former Boston City Architect George A. Clough. Clough did his fair share of grumbling later when the building committee scotched the 250-foot dome they had encouraged him to study and restudy and for which they refused to pay him. Clough unsuccessfully sued the county for what he considered to be due recompense.

What was accomplished finally, after expenditure of a scandalous $2,530,000 and a protracted and rancorous period of construction, stands today in Pemberton Square, described even when just completed as "the most thoroughly concealed public building within our knowledge" (pl. 62). One is forced by the proximity of the surrounding structures to view it at close range, and the predominant impression is of an attempt to awe by quantity. The building is a mountain of Massachusetts granite, 450 by 190 feet; it contains courthouse space, four open-air courtyards for ventilation, and a Great Hall that serves as a public connector through the building. This colossal space (pl. 2), even without its dome, rises from below a parade of allegorical figures sculpted by Domingo Mora through a series of balustraded balconies, colonnades, and arcades to culminate in a vaulted ceiling, decorated with frescoes, which is five stories above the ground. (The space is so unhappily lighted, however, that much of its grandeur is lost.)

By 1909 the building already was judged too small, and Clough was rehired to enlarge it. His solution was to design two additional stories in the form of an enormous mansard roof (pl. 63), interrupted by raised center and end pavilions. While this change brought more integrity to the building's massing, it also had the uncanny effect of casting it in an older style—Second Empire Baroque. If the building was a bit *retardataire* when it was new, the enlargement put it some forty years out of fashion.

As impressive as it is, the Boston Courthouse is not a very good piece of architecture. Its massing is confused, partly because its articulated pavilions are too small to serve as visual anchors, and, even more, because it is overly layered horizontally. The principal cornice, usually the crowning feature of a Classical building, is close to the center of the façade, and it is just one of a myriad of horizontal bands that divide the building into a wedding cake of horizontal layers. Each layer, moreover, is endowed with a unique window treatment—in fact, there is scarcely a motif encompassing more than a single story that might serve to unite a package of disparate parts. This could be composed of slices of many different buildings that happened to fit together. It is, in a word, *ponderous*.

At issue here is a historical problem dealt with by a succession of architects after 1850 or so: What should a tall building look like? Tall buildings (over six stories) became technically possible before there was an aesthetic solution to them. Earliest responses produced the unsatisfying formula of layered floors. This problem was not adequately solved until Boston-born Louis Henri Sullivan and others working in Chicago in the late eighties learned to express height in new poetic ways free of layering. But the way had already been pointed out by Henry Hobson Richardson, working in Boston, who, before his death in the very year Clough began designing this courthouse, had achieved international recognition for his new vision of American architecture.

Richardson

Architects should not be made the convenience of contractors.
—HENRY HOBSON RICHARDSON

9   Hampden County Courthouse, Springfield (By permission of The Houghton Library, Harvard University)

That the art of one man, even in his brief lifetime, should come to captivate virtually an entire generation of architects and provide Main Street America with so much uniform architecture, is but one measure of the enormous accomplishment of Henry Hobson Richardson (1838–1886). He was our first architectural giant, and was regarded in Europe as a great architect and in America as a great American. The author of Trinity Church, Boston, was revered by his contemporaries in virtually every state, and they copied his style without ever fully grasping the more fundamental dimensions of his work. And he was studied by ensuing generations who, although they discarded his style, made buildings of power and dignity because they understood his approach to things.

His was an art of affirmation. He affirmed average American institutions by recasting them in dignified new forms, generating new prototypes for small town public libraries, train stations, average houses, commercial and educational buildings, and courthouses. He built two courthouses; the one in Springfield came early in his career and the other, in Pittsburgh (which he considered his finest building), came at the very end.

Richardson was born on a plantation in Louisiana, was graduated from Harvard in 1859, and was only the second American to enter the course of architecture at the Ecole des Beaux-Arts in Paris, where he arrived just as Union gunboats were blockading southern ports. Being cut off from his family's financial support, he worked his way through long years of school. He practiced briefly in New York, and then, since almost all his commissions were in Massachusetts, moved his office to Brookline in 1874. In the dozen years that followed, he did work so fundamentally calm and accessible that he could be said to have effectively closed the Victorian period in American architecture.

He was, for all that, no modern. He was happy to build in the eternal way, in stone. He never experimented with new technologies, nor did he work in nonhistorical styles. His stylistic point of departure was French Romanesque architecture from the Middle Ages, but this physically huge man was drawn to it because it was a massive, strong, and rational architecture that was still richly ornamented. He did not find his style until the middle of his career; his earlier buildings form a history of his search for a style in harmony with his ideas of rational planning, monumental dignity, and calm surfaces of subdued color—the very antithesis of much Victorian American architecture.

His Hampden County Courthouse in Springfield (1871) is generally regarded as the first statement of both the stylistic and constructional ideas that were to dominate his mature work. The building is solid, rising from the earth on a flared, or battered base, and is in a single material, rock-faced Monson granite. This is uniformly light gray in color, and a lighter version is used for the understated trim. (Remember that a common picturesque ideal was polychromy, the use of many materials for their varied color.) It is a nearly symmetrical building, contrary to the tastes of the times, and the second-floor balcony to the left is balanced by the thin slot window to the right—Richardson's concession to the picturesque love of asymmetry. One enters the building through a recessed porch behind three powerful arches—a huge arch at the entry was to become Richardson's "signature." Rising above the front façade is the building's dominant feature—a machicolated medieval tower, perfectly Picturesque, showing that even for Richardson a tower was an indispensable part of a monument. Norcross Brothers of Worcester, who were to build most of Richardson's buildings, were the contractors for this courthouse, which cost $214,068 and was finally dedicated in 1874.

The original building (fig. 9) gracefully fused the tower with the main mass of the building by means of a steeply pitched hipped roof and several tall medieval French dormers which rose from behind a crenellated parapet. Quite unfortunately, alterations between 1908 and 1912 by Richardson's own successor firm (Shepley, Rutan, and Coolidge) were so severe and insensitive of the building's integrity that Richardson's intent is lost. The roof and dormers were stripped away, the original graceful double staircase was replaced by a straight-shot flight, and the tall second story was divided into two floors that bisected the stately front windows with a heavy horizontal band (pl. 56).

Eleven months after he received the Springfield commission, Richardson was notified that he had won a design competition for the new Trinity Church in Boston. It was the construction of this building that vaulted Richardson into national attention, and it was the style and material of it that set the appearance of the typical "Richardsonian" building. He himself frequently repeated thereafter the two-colored stone combination: pale pink for the walls and brownstone for the trim and marquetry (geometric ornament integral with the surface of the stone). Most of the public buildings done for the rest of his career would prove to be variants of this basic sedate color combination, and of this freely adapted Romanesque style.

Richardson died of Bright's disease at forty-nine, which must certainly be considered mid-career. The work of his last few years marked a clear transformation from his overtly historically based style to something more abstractly related to qualities of the material he used. His massive Marshall Field Wholesale Store (1885) in Chicago, almost devoid of ornamentation, was a solid rectangle filling an entire block whose single-color stone walls rose through seven stories, articulated only by the diminishing sizes of the stone blocks and the sheer poetry of the way openings were made for windows. And his Allegheny County Courthouse and Jail (1883–1888) in Pittsburgh, having similar qualities, pointed the way, in its gargantuan simplicity and expressiveness, to a future body of work that was not to be. The jail, particularly, is said by historian James O'Gorman to rank "among the world's finest examples of stereometric art." The expectations of this move to abstraction went unrealized by either Richardson or his followers, but the buildings of his middle career, being widely published, found immediate favor. With astonishing rapidity, American architects abandoned other styles and began emulating at least the appearance of Richardson's buildings.

Massachusetts built one courthouse a year in the five years following Richardson's death in 1886; four of these are overtly Richardsonian in appearance and the other is in its massing, but not in its style. They are but five of the tens of thousands of buildings built in virtually every town in the country in the twenty years following his death which are derived from his personal accomplishments.

In many ways, the Hampshire County Courthouse (pl. 30) is more Richardsonian than the "real thing" in neighboring Springfield. Its massing is nearly identical, and it happily still has its roof and dormers. Architect Henry F. Kilbourn paid homage to Richardson by casting this version of Springfield's courthouse in typical light rock-faced granite with window surrounds, stringcourses, and decorative stonework in brownstone. The triple-arched entry on squat muscular columns, the calm surfaces and simple massing, the breadth of proportion in the tower—all these were learned from Richardson.

The building was built between 1885 and 1887 by Bartlett Brothers of Whately for a cost of just under $100,000. Of interest here are the contemporary descriptions of the original interiors. They reveal a woodworking program whereby each major space received furniture and decorative woodwork of a different wood: dark cherry for the registry of deeds, ash for the register of probate, and so forth. All offices also had glazed doors with titles cut into the glass, and the building boasted good ventilation, central steam heating, generous public washrooms, and newfangled electric lighting.

The Superior Courtroom (pl. 15) is the centerpiece of the building. It is a grand theatrical space whose furniture, benches, wainscot, and railings are all of carved golden oak (pl. 33), as are the front hall and staircase that lead to it. In its coverage of the dedication ceremonies (December 20, 1887), the *Northampton Courier* reported that "about one-third of the room is behind the railing which holds the lawyers and their victims," who had the honor of sitting under a large ceiling cove (pl. 32) adorned with colorful frescoes and "dark Egyptian stencils" by F. D. Cordis of Holyoke. A bell cast by Paul Revere, which had hung in the demolished courthouse of 1822, was now displayed in the 1887 building.

The very next year (1888), Essex County decided to enlarge its Salem Courthouse. Architects Holman K. Wheeler and W. W. Northend of Lynn ended up spending $147,115.13 in the process of quadrupling the size of the 1861 structure, and they thoroughly Richardsonized it (fig. 10). Working in brick, in deference to the older structure, they so altered its exterior as to leave little of its original Italianate character. The balustrades, pediment, hooded window moldings, and quoins were stripped away as so much architectural claptrap, and Romanesque arches were substituted at the windows (pl. 75). Rough granite stringcourses and trim were applied, and, most conspicuously, the original entry bay was masked by a new Romanesque pavilion, the entire ground floor of which is a ponderous entry arch standing on Richardsonian bundles of stout columns.

The addition itself, free of the constraints of renovation, is much grander and more successful. Its rear parts resemble in massing nothing so much as a medieval French castle, standing cheek-by-jowl with the chaste 1841 Greek Revival temple. Bizarre juxtapositions, one of the ironies and great delights of the American Picturesque, here foreshadowed Disneyworld by nearly a century. And, of course, the lack of a tower was rectified by building one in Richardsonian proportions. On the whole, this is good architecture, conceived, as Richardson would have it, not only for the sake of its picturesque exterior, but as a composition of spaces both functional and grand.

The true glory of this building is its law library. The courtrooms have their own grandeur (pl. 74)—tall spaces with beautifully paneled oak woodwork and furniture, and the splendid coffered and multidomed ceilings (pl. 76), but for the sheer power of monumental space, nothing equals the library (pl. 12). The floor is a solid plane of herringbone brick; portraits of noted jurors are everywhere, and the sensuous use of oak throughout the building reaches a climax in this space in the kingly furniture and paneled wings of bookshelving which surround it on two levels. The second-level balcony, accessible through a winding stair which forms a pinnacled turret on the exterior, is sur-

10   Salem Courthouse, Essex County (Keller & Peet Associates)

rounded with a delicate swelling wrought-iron railing and is interrupted only by the truly enormous arch that opens onto an inglenook. This last is an entire room whose sole function is to contain an equally enormous fireplace, whose chimney is so large and raised on bunches of columns that it allows a group to sit inside on easy chairs! The ceiling is vaulted and carried on curved ribs springing from brackets shaped like winged cherubs. But the force of this monumental space is so great that the ceiling seems only a thin membrane that is being restrained by straps as it swells outward. The whole space, finally, is suffused with daylight from a long crowning skylight.

Although a similar spatial conception is not found in the Fall River Courthouse (1889), there is a similar effect of strength from the exterior (fig. 11). This building, too, has antecedents in medieval fortresses and, like Salem, attempts to speak of the unassailable strength and safety of the law. Here the material is more late-Richardsonian—pure granite with no overtly coloristic touches (the lesson of calm surfaces was learned). But the irregularly picturesque composition of volumes—pavilions, dormers, porches, swelling turrets, chimneys, cupolas, and, of course, the tower—is pure Victorian excess, and pure delight. This must be considered, for all its Richardsonian style, still a High Romantic building. The overscaled tower is placed right at the leading corner where it monopolizes attention. It derives both its compositional predominance and its general detailing—pyramidal roof rising from four equal corner turrets connected by four-arched bands—directly from Richardson's Pittsburgh Courthouse. It rises from a battered base, and its windows, divided by stone mullions, as well as its entryway of receding arches in short columns, are quotations from Pittsburgh.

The architect of the Fall River Courthouse was Robert H. Black of New Bedford, and the contractors were the Darling Brothers of Fall River. The cornerstone, which contained among its official documents a mint set of 1889 U.S. coins, was laid with Masonic ceremonies on August 8, 1899, and the building was completed in 1891 at a cost of $181,016. In 1931 an addition was made on the north end to house the registry of deeds and the law library. Although this annex is not wholly unconsonant with the Richardsonian building, the matching stonework becomes brick just around the corner.

And the grandest of them all is the Taunton Courthouse, by architect Frank Irving Cooper. Resembling a sort of junior state capitol more than a county courthouse, this building is surely the most monumental of its type in the Commonwealth (pl. 50). It, too, bears more than a passing resemblance to Pittsburgh, but it was based on the published scheme with which Richardson won the Pittsburgh design competition, and not on the scheme that was actually built. This unbuilt scheme had a central gabled bay and a tower rising from within the roof, neither of which ended up in the actual building. Taunton's cornerstone was laid on June 30, 1892, long after both schemes were

11 Fall River Courthouse, Bristol County (Keller & Peet Associates)

widely known, so it is an example of a work consciously modeled after another architect's unrealized work. Its rough granite, near-symmetry, gabled center pavilion with triple-arched central windows and arched entry, its French dormers topped with bulbous finials, and its soaring turreted tower are all practically quotations from the master.

A major departure, however, is that a grand copper dome culminating in the Flame of Truth is substituted for Richardson's pointed tower roof. This dome crowns a vast shaft of space inside (pl. 51), which rises from the ground floor through the full height of the tower. This is the centerpiece of a carefully orchestrated sequence of spaces designed to instill in visitors, jurors, and miscreants alike a sense of the majesty of the law. Visitors arrive at the courtroom by an elaborate series of staircases (pl. 3) which begin in the rotunda under the dome (pl. 4) and pass through and into spaces richly endowed with carvings, mosaics, frescoes, and Tiffany lamps. Prisoners, on the other hand, are brought from dark subterranean holding cells (pl. 52) through back corridors (pl. 53) and up a narrow flight of stairs (pl. 54) to emerge into the splendor of the courtroom (pl. 55) already at its center and face-to-face with the judge, who is sitting between two immutably stout columns and under a triple-arched opening.

Here, for the first time, an architect has taken advantage of axial planning, dramatic use of light, changes in level, and the persuasive force of archetypal forms to create a work of functional art that embodies the majestic authority of Justice. All this is because of Richardson. By his example both the art and professional dignity of architecture was obtained, and America saw new visions of how all its institutions—from the most humble to the most grand—might be housed anew with sufficient scale and breadth of vision to match the challenges of a new century.

12   Brockton Courthouse, Plymouth County (Keller & Peet Associates)

Academic Eclecticism

The scale is Roman and it will have
to be sustained.
—CHARLES FOLLEN MCKIM

There is in architecture after 1890 a new sense of scale and rectitude heretofore unseen. Continued urbanization and the growth of government had produced by the last decade of the century an America unprecedented in wealth, ebullience, and global influence. This developing urban empire seemed to require an architecture suited to its power, its wealth, its bigness. Our great cities were thought the equals of Paris, London, or Rome. By careful study and imitation of the major historical styles with which these cities were adorned, New York might outstrip London; Chicago, Paris; or Washington,

Rome. American architects could embody, could indeed *promote*, a New World challenging the glories of the Old.

Victorian architecture came to be regarded as excessively fussy and naive, drowned in a sea of misguided invention, perversion of materials, and cloying picturesqueness. The "fault" of the Victorians was thought to be a fundamental lack of familiarity with the buildings they supposedly had tried to emulate. Most earlier architects had experienced European buildings neither in person nor in photographs, and a more scholarly knowledge of great buildings was assumed to lead to an architecture as grand and correct as the originals. The new schools of architecture in the country, developed only in the last thirty-five years of the century, were the perfect vehicles for transmitting this scholarly knowledge of the Classical orders, rules of composition and detailing, and, in short, "right" and "wrong." They, it was hoped, could save architects from a Vitruvian purgatory to which most Victorians (Richardson and a few others were excepted) had been consigned.

It was an age of eclecticism in architecture, of stylistic pluralism. Any style was admissible, as long as it was used for the appropriate building type (e.g., Gothic for a church, Roman Classicism for a museum) and detailed according to rules of propriety prescribed by academicians. Wealthy people and institutions found this an architecture they could easily understand and one that reinforced their identity as people of culture. It suited the purposes of the powerful.

There was even a debutante ball held for this academic eclecticism in Chicago. The World's Columbian Exposition in 1893 was housed in the first totally planned architectural fantasy of Imperial Rome in the country. Most of the buildings were designed by eastern architects and were enormous, white, and uniformly Classical. They were aligned on either side of a vast reflecting pool and were adorned with statuary and ornament. And, to the amazement of all, they were electrically floodlighted at night.

The Classical impulse was most closely associated with the development of city centers, and generated a movement known as the "City Beautiful" whose purpose was to order and classicize urban America. The Columbian Exposition gave a first glimpse of an urban space in which the designer, not profits and politics, controlled all—ordered buildings, streets, plantings, plazas, fountains, and the like. Hardly a city did not feel the pressure to make itself a City Beautiful, tricked out with statuary and bursting with civic pride. Architect Daniel ["Make no little plans"] Burnham of Chicago, who had coordinated planning of the Exposition, was instrumental in new plans for many cities, including San Francisco, Cleveland, Chicago, and, most important, the nation's capital. The axial vastness of Major L'Enfant's 1791 Baroque scheme for Washington had been seriously compromised by Picturesque alterations (e.g., a train station in the middle of a Romantic garden where the Mall now is). In 1901 the MacMillan

Commission, chaired by Burnham, began redesigning the city and succeeded in making it the City Beautiful par excellence we know today, adorned with a multitude of enormous white Classical buildings. Thereafter, monumental Academic Classicism was almost required for governmental buildings.

The influence of McKim, Mead, and White, Architects of New York, was to be unparalleled. Both Charles Follen McKim (1847–1909) and Stanford White (1853–1906) had worked for Richardson as young men. As is typical in architecture, the most talented do not stay around to inherit their employer's firm, but rather cast out on their own. Made restless by their own astonishing talent, they teamed up and, with William Rutherford Mead, founded our first large professional architectural firm. Their first major commission, the Boston Public Library (1887), set in play a new standard for Classicism which came to dominate the next half-century of public buildings. Likewise, the work of Bostonian Ralph Adams Cram (1863–1942) and his partner Bertram Grosvenor Goodhue (1869–1924) was influential in Gothic circles, and their All Saints' Church in the Ashmont section of Dorchester was as catalytic as the library. Sacred and secular, the influence of these two protean Boston buildings was immense.

Courthouses all became up-scale Classical monuments, usually Roman by virtue of association with Roman law, but frequently grandiose Greek as well. The city of Lowell's pushing its old courthouse back to accommodate a new Roman vision is the essence of the movement. This occurred in 1898, when the ability of new architects in proper Classicism was more assured. An earlier effort at Brockton is interesting because, although it is more naive as a piece of City Beautiful Classicism, it is still pronouncedly Richardsonian in its massing.

So much of the Brockton Courthouse (fig. 12), designed in 1893 by J. Williams Beal, has been stripped away after having been allowed to decay that it is difficult to see the City Beautiful in it at all. Nevertheless, its current Richardsonian appearance—its sloping roughstone base, entry arch, solid and blocky proportions, and low hipped roof—was once adorned with a sufficient quantity of classicizing elements to give a hint of its having its origins in the early work of McKim, Mead, and White. It originally had a fine cornice and Classical balustrade, and its roof hips terminated in spirelike copper pinnacles, like the Boston Public Library. The whole was topped by a delicate open cupola. The cupola, pinnacles, balustrade, and cornice are gone now, the last replaced by an awkward, thin, snap-on aluminum fascia. But other Classical elements remain: brick quoins, Renaissance archways, a Palladian window, the scallop shell niche heads, decorative roundels, and the bas-relief band at the top. The interior still abounds with Classical details—the gorgeously carved wood overmantle and ribbed plaster vaulted ceiling in the small courtroom (pl. 59), for example. It is unfortunate that a great deal of this woodwork has been painted over.

Lawrence, too, participated in the City Beautiful movement when its Italianate courthouse was enlarged and reworked in 1900 by local architect George G. Adams (1850–1932), who also enlarged the neighboring city hall twenty-three years later. The original courthouse, still visible today as the rear portion of the present building, had stood in its own small park which was filled by a new building, grandiosely Classical and based loosely on the urban work of Palladio. Here, again, the referent is Italian Renaissance palaces. A rusticated masonry ground floor surmounted by two grand stories in smooth red brick is topped by an attic balustrade. Onto this dignified exterior is grafted a monumental pedimented portico flanked by pairs of colossal order columns standing on plinth blocks. This dramatically reinforces the main entry, which was shifted to Appleton Street so that the building no longer fronted on the Common. The whole composition was once again even further monumentalized by a crowning Classical tower, now sadly removed.

More of Roman scale is found inside. The center of the building is occupied by a grand stairhall, roofed over by a domed skylight carried on enormous arches and pendentives—whose origins lie in the great baths of imperial Rome (pl. 5, 26, 27). The use of large-scale Roman prototypes for public buildings in turn-of-the-century America typifies the City Beautiful movement. The noble ideal that urban streets and public places might be enriched by uniformly good architecture—the beginning of urban design—first came to fruition then. Herein lay the first general recognition that buildings acted in concert to give character to cities, and that an architect's responsibility transcends the individual building to encompass concern for the quality of the *city*.

Completed in 1898 at a cost of $370,000, Lowell's courthouse is a much better example of the City Beautiful under full steam. Here is a truly monumental building, all in stone, correct in its detailing, imposing in its scale (pls. 8, 68). In public buildings the sine qua non of the period was a grand pedimented colonnade across the front, frequently, as here, raised on an arcaded lower story (recall Pittsfield). Here the Roman Ionic columns and cornice are imposing, partly because they are properly designed, and ennoble a properly detailed Renaissance palace, of which the rusticated base, use of keystones, pedimented window surrounds, and balustrade are all indications. Herein lies a new statement about the law: it was associated through its architectural personality with other new governmental buildings around the Commonwealth and nation, as well as with that which is timeless and immutable about things Roman, both legal and architectural. And besides, as Walter Kilham observed, "all building committees like columns." What's more, it became something of a necessity in cities to resort to deliberately over-scaled Classical architecture in order to reassert a building's importance in the hierarchy of large and clamorous urban structures, commercial and cultural alike.

When the courthouse complex in Salem took its next step down Federal Street in 1909, its building committee obviously liked columns, too, because they bought six of them (Ionic, carrying a monumental pediment). The 1909 courthouse is similar to the one in Lowell in many regards, and differs principally in style—Athenian rather than Roman. There never was a Greek Empire, but if there had been, its buildings would have looked like this. Perhaps architect Clarence Blackall (1857–1942) of Boston, who also designed the Wilbur and Colonial theatres, the Copley Plaza Hotel, and the Winthrop Building in Boston (this last was the first use of a steel frame for a high-rise structure in Boston), deferred to the 1841 Greek Revival courthouse with which the row begins. But it sits in such overscaled grandeur that it seems out of place on what would otherwise be principally a narrow residential street.

The Eclectics loved almost all styles, as long as they were done properly and with taste (but they not always were). They worked in them all. Particularly in New England, correct if overblown Georgian Revival styles were deemed appropriate for certain building types, particularly those with genuine colonial antecedents. Georgian Revival was popularized, again by McKim, Mead, and White's use of it for new buildings at Harvard and Radcliffe. By the 1930s there were Georgian gymnasia, restrooms, banks, and gas stations. (There were also Spanish colonial, Gothic, Tudor, Renaissance, and Romanesque gas stations.) In 1932 the last Eclectic Superior courthouse was built in Massachusetts, in Greenfield. The Franklin County Courthouse (fig. 13), by architects Frank King and Bernard Dirks, is ostensibly Classical in mien, and because it is made of brick it appears somewhat Georgian. It, too, has a colossal-order temple front at the entry and many Classical details, but they are from a mixed bag of sources. The quoins are Georgian, the end windows in the front façade are Adamesque/Federal, the pediments at the doors and the double-cross mullions in the upper windows are Roman, the columns are Tuscan topped with Greco-Egyptian capitals, the little volutes along the parapet are Renaissance, and so forth. Here is a kind of toy box of architectural parts. All of this confusion has a certain grace and charm, although it is not the detail one notices most about the building, but its form. It is a box. Here is an edifice shaped by its method of construction—a steel frame—with a flat roof, a thin skin, and style-giving pieces, not integral with the mass and structure as, for example, at Lowell, but rather treated as appliqué. One need only recall Old Plymouth to see Greenfield as proof of the longevity of that basic American type, the decorated box.

The interior is dignified by rich materials (pl. 25), marble among them, and skilled workmanship. The judge sits in front of a sort of

13 Franklin County Courthouse, Greenfield (Keller & Peet Associates)

Chippendale bookcase (pl. 24), and the courtroom doorways carry full Renaissance pediments on scrolled volutes.

The flood of buildings since the Civil War dried to a trickle following 1929, and did not begin to revive until around 1950 as the country rode out depression, war, and recession. By mid-century the need to build was severe; America occupied antiquated buildings. The factories that built the planes that won the war stood ready to re-tool for making buildings sorely needed.

Modernism

Without a peep they move in!—even
though the glass box appals them all.
—TOM WOLFE

At the turn of the century, elements of both European and American society began to apply pressure for a "new art," reflective of modern conditions, free of stylistic links to the past, and expressive of that which made society *unlike* rather than like its progenitors. Academic revivals, constantly defining the present in terms of the past, grew trivial and spiritually tiresome. Europe responded at first with Art Nouveau ("the New Art"), derived in part from an abstraction of asymmetrical curving forms found in organic nature. This was possible in the general climate of ever-broadening rules for artistic syntax fomented by the Impressionists in painting and music, which allowed increasing deviation from historical precedent. The tendencies toward abstraction in the late work of Richardson served for Louis Sullivan in Chicago as a catalyst to promote a substantively original and polemical sort of architecture, in turn part of the fertile ground from which flowered the brilliant work of Frank Lloyd Wright. This genealogy of original work was buried by the fervor for historical styles that existed after the 1893 Chicago Exposition, but it found enthusiastic support among the architectural avant-garde in Holland and Germany.

Art Nouveau went through a series of regional permutations in Europe (e.g., the Vienna Secession, Expressionism in Germany, the work of Charles Rennie Mackintosh in Scotland). The Chicago Tribune Tower design competition (1922) elicited entries from around the world, which were published, and although a *retardataire* Gothic skyscraper was built, it was the modern European entries that proved to be more influential. Even Raymond Hood, the winner, was converted to modern design by the second-place entry of Finnish architect Eliel Saarinen, whose tower was devoid of overtly historical ornament and rose through a series of zigguratlike stepbacks to an ornamented crown. When designers began to apply the active geometricized ornamental patterns and crystalline forms that dominated the 1925 Paris *Exposition Internationale des Arts Décoratifs et Industriels Modernes* to stepped-back building forms, the result was a new futuristic architecture called Art Deco. This was an accessible modernism inspired by the wonders of the immediate world: jazz, electricity, phonographs, cinema, flight, and *speed.* When, in the Thirties this became tempered and slickened by the application of aerodynamic styling (originated by transportation engineers), to designed objects, everything from towers to toasters looked as if it were traveling at two hundred miles an hour.

During the Thirties, even the government got into the act. While not abandoning Classicism, it accepted certain new attitudes about pared-down and smoothed-out styling, and in its attempt to stimulate a depression-ridden economy through major building campaigns, it generated a new sort of Depression Classicism. Characterized by a streamlining of traditional Classical (and patriotic) motifs, it was capable of producing monumental public buildings that could still speak with authority. There is a courtroom in the Brockton Courthouse in this style, whose space is defined by thin fluted pilasters of no overt Classical order, ranged around wall planes with wood panel and plaster infill between the pilasters. All the woodwork, although derived from Classical forms, is geometric and abstract, with such pieces as the bookshelving behind the judge stepped back toward the top in an Art Deco fashion.

This judge's backdrop at Brockton is dominated by a form remarkably similar to the entire shape of the "new" Suffolk Courthouse in Boston, built in 1938 from plans by Desmond and Lord. Here is an entire Moderne skyscraper (Thirties styling). This twenty-story tower (pl. 62), appended to the end of the earlier Boston courthouse is mostly unornamented on its white brick exterior, deriving its presence from its setback form, making it a country cousin of the era's monarchs: Manhattan's Chrysler and Empire State buildings. However, unlike them, the Suffolk Courthouse was not the product of an effervescent, wealthy, and self-confident age, but of a decade of limited means and growing global conflict which sorely tried the ability of a democratic government to maintain an even course.

A governmental need to display, with limited means, traditional symbols of itself is here everywhere apparent. The aesthetic is one of spaces defined by thin planes and thin ornament, derived from Classicism, intended to convey the presence of governmental authority: fluted pilaster panels, bas-relief stars and eagles, light fixtures like Roman fasces, and so forth. The courtroom and conference room of the Supreme Judicial Court (pls. 64, 65), for example, are dignified assemblies of these parts wrought thin and flat in wood paneling, although from this it is possible to get a sense, not only of modernity, but of the dwindling availability of skilled craftsmen capable of executing more substantial traditional work.

It was, in fact, the replacement of craftsmen by machines that radically reshaped architecture everywhere, and this was not simply a reluctant acceptance of the inevitable, but a conscious embrace of the machine because it seemed to make something as profound as a new social order possible.

Modernism (history will supply a better name) began in Germany and Holland with a manifesto and a radical social program. Out of the debris of World War I arose the new idea that architecture was a latent political force that could actually *create* society and not just reflect it. In the confused postwar German society, a union of artists, designers, and architects was founded that, in 1919 at Weimar, set up an institute to teach these disciplines afresh. The school was called the Bauhaus, and it taught that there was but one way to rehouse the population of industrial Europe with at least minimally acceptable standards of hygiene and comfort, and that was by transforming the very industry that had been an instrument of oppression into the instrument of salvation. The penchant of the machine for mass production was to be harnessed to the need for new buildings so perfectly made that their inhabitants might finally transcend the past altogether and, in a glorious new future, live free from want, ignorance, and the tyranny of old politics.

The teaching of history was banished. Gone were notions of style and ornament and concern for the appearance of forms shaped by anything other than necessity. From buildings to lightbulbs to teakettles, all objects of human utility were remade in forms purported to be derived strictly from their roles, from funciton. And this functionalism produced objects of beguiling abstraction. Preferred materials were industrial ones—concrete, steel, glass—and these rendered walls and roofs into flat pure planes of white stucco or sheer curtains of glass. Space, set free from bearing walls by frame construction, became continuous flow rather than a collection of rooms, and that continuity merged indoors with outdoors separated only by plate glass. Delight in these buildings was the product of an intellectual appreciation of the forces that shaped them, more than a visual and emotional pleasure.

Early Modern buildings share many characteristics that gave them a uniform appearance, and, as the rest of the world adopted functionalist architecture, it was codified into a set of rules, accompanied by philosophical slogans ("form follows funciton"; "less is more"). It was at least partially successful; it did, for example, provide improved workers' housing on a vast scale. But in its rejection of familiarity—ornament, archetypal forms, parts that admitted the existence of human idiosyncrasy, or materials that admitted the existence of climate—it threw out the baby with the bathwater. With all the positive aspects of history discarded, we were left with a fairly monotonous way of making buildings whereby a boilerhouse might resemble a church, or a church, a boilerhouse. Furthermore, mass-produced functionalist architecture was founded on the ability to accommodate the masses, in housing or offices, for example, and the individual became increasingly lost in the collective.

In its pure form, this architectural language proved to be not rich enough to satisfy our needs to speak through buildings, or to take visual delight in them. Americans had difficulty with what billed itself as a largely intellectualized and nonemotional art, and from the beginning there were problems in using this architecture to make both monumental public structures and urban public space that people felt comfortable inhabiting. An architecture invented for workers' housing was not necessarily applicable to all other purposes.

One reaction was to ignore it. There has always been a modest amount of historical and picturesque work, some justified in part on the argument of contextualism; the context of a new building requires an appropriate stylistic response. The county and town of Nantucket, for example, building its combined municipal and courthouse building (fig. 14) as late as 1967, required (as it does of all new buildings on the island) that it adhere to a code that regulates architectural character. This rather plain building (pl. 58), by associated architects Tallman, Drake, and Guay, defers to its context by having a few decorative touches that transform the ordinary two-story brick structure into one reminiscent of Federal Style architecture not inappropriate to Nantucket. Its basic form, however, is neither Federal nor particularly monumental—it actually bears a greater resemblance to early brick textile mills than to any other specific building type. It has a doorway graced by a fanlight recalling early nineteenth-century residences and an obligatory, if underscaled, cupola, which more than anything else marks this building as a civic monument.

Modernist architects diverged in a number of directions from the mainstream trying to rectify a perceived lack of visual and experiential richness. The most conservative response was to animate buildings by making the structure, the part of a building that holds the building up, into its ornament. This produces a self-revelatory kind of architecture that signifies nothing more meaningful to society than that the building is held up by this or that means. It creates no sense of order qualitatively greater than its own physical presence. Similarly self-revelatory in elevating what must be in a building anyway to the position of appearing as its reason to exist, is the High Tech approach, in which the plumbing and mechanical engineering—the ductwork, diffusers, piping, and valves—are exposed to view and painted in such a way that it is supposed to ornament and justify the building. Good examples in Massachusetts are the new Boston Five Cent Savings Bank (structural revelation) or the new Wellesley College Science Center, which is an exaltation of the technology of exhaust. A more germane example is the 1981 addition, by Phineas Alpers, on the rear of the 1909 Salem Courthouse which equates county government with cast-in-place concrete columns and beams.

14   Nantucket Courthouse, Nantucket County (Keller & Peet Associates)

A third enrichment of dogmatic Modernism is abstract expression in architecture, in which abstract forms and the visual forces between them are used to express content and its value. Here the possibility of monumental urban work is greater, as Kallmann and McKinnell's Boston City Hall will attest. The fact that abstract expressionist forms are subjectively received can permit a number of interpretations, which allows Boston City Hall to be seen as a great fortress protecting corrupt city officials from an outraged public, as well as the more intended noble incarnation of the proper relationship between a variety of civic offices and the citizenry which legitimizes them.

A final and more pervasive ramification of Modernism is the formalist school in which buildings exist for the sake of making shapes, sometimes smoothly geometric (the Kennedy Library, for example), and sometimes articulated and boxlike. And it is here that the story comes full circle: our most persevering architectural type, the decorated box, has proven to be as modern as the latest age. But whereas previously one could apply overt historical ornament to the box, Modernist architects could only couch their ornament in terms of something that had to be there anyway—structural and mechanical parts, window mullions, sunscreens, exhaust louvers, and the like—to achieve a decorative effect of some visual interest.

Something of the more coolly geometric sort occurred when architects Drummey, Rosane and Anderson renovated the courthouse in Northampton in 1977. The Georgian Hall of Records (1931) of architects Karl S. Putnam and Frank S. Stuart was expanded (pls. 31, 16), and an old hotel garage across the street was turned into a new registry of deeds by reclothing it in concrete block and tinted plate glass in a single plane. This planar exterior wall seems to have no dimensional thickness at all, leaving the simple geometric shape of the building defined by a smooth tight skin.

Hampden County outgrew its Richardson courthouse in Springfield and in 1973 created a court complex by building a new $17 million Hall of Justice beside the older building. Designed by Eduardo Catalano (who was also the architect of a downtown suburban shopping center in the same city called Baystate West), the building is an enormous concrete and tinted glass box, virtually indistinguishable from a new high school, a clinic, or, more specifically, the same architect's Stratton Student Center at M.I.T. It contains twenty courtrooms described by Probate Judge Frank Plazcek as "austere but not cold," and its exterior is imposing, partly because of the scale of its blank concrete surfaces and long glazed strips, and partly because the bulk of the building overhangs pedestrians approaching the building at ground level. The façade is animated only by the exit stair towers, which rise to a height greater than the rest of the façade. Altogether, this is at best a banal building that makes little effort to say something positive about the relationship between society and the law.

The 1974 high-rise Cambridge Courthouse and County Building is not good architecture either, but one admires its attempt to articulate a variety of spaces and functions within. Even when one is told that the Springfield building is a courthouse, one still struggles to find an announcement of what lies inside. Knowing that the Cambridge building is a courthouse at least allows one to try assigning court-related functions to the variety of forms that animate its surfaces (fig. 15). There are, for example, those blank darker-colored boxes that project from two sides of the tower. One might reasonably expect that they contain some specialized function, or that something special is going on at the level marked by a recessed red band, or in the uppermost four stories of the tower, wrapped in a bricolage of concrete sticks and translucent glazing. The tower rises from a wider podium of four stories, which would appear to also contain special functions. This podium is half of an unrealized base structure, with an open central courtyard, which would have occupied the site of the Bulfinch courthouse across the street, scheduled for demolition as part of this project. (The old courthouse was preserved and renovated by Graham Gund Associates, Inc., of Cambridge for a new life as Bulfinch Square, a complex of offices, theaters, restaurants, and other public functions.)

One could rationally construct, in fact, a completely incorrect reading of these forms by assuming that the courtrooms, the most important public spaces in the building, would occupy the special podium at the lower levels where public access is facilitated; that the solid blank boxes higher up, with their absence of windows and their somewhat brooding hooded openings might logically contain jail cells; or, because the tops of tall buildings are always special places, that the offices of persons of exalted rank would be there; or perhaps that a cafeteria for employees occupied this space.

But the building, designed by Edward J. Tedesco of Winchester, is not explicit enough for us to "read" it with any certainty. In fact, the lowermost floors are occupied by the bureaucracies attending the court clerks, county commissioners, the district attorney, and the law library; while courtrooms, sandwiched in between mechanical floors, occupy the windowless saddlebags somewhere in the middle of the structure, and prisoners are placed in windowless cells at the top of the building where the views are best and as far from the sally port as possible. There are other ambiguities here. There is an attempt to "decorate" the façades with concrete sun-baffles, but these are given equal treatment on all four faces of the building even though the sun strikes them at different angles and intensities or, on the north, not at all. Half of the sixteen courtrooms in the building are round (pl. 18) (their space focusing on the defendant rather than on the judge or jury), and lighted by oppressively glowing round ceilings, and yet there is no hint of round spaces on the exterior. The lowermost story of the podium is treated as a visual foundation for the

15 Cambridge Courthouse, Middlesex County (Keller & Peet Associates)

whole structure by having far fewer windows, and yet it appears that the monolithic concrete superstructure of the building is sitting on a loose pile of tiny sugarcubelike stone blocks. Surely here is a perversion of materials and a confusion of decorative patterns as heinous as anything Modernists might have accused earlier ages of having perpetrated.

History may prove the 1980s to be the beginning of another chapter dealing with the reestablishment of discarded architectural traditions—conventions generated for sound reasons are likely to reassert their proper role in the general scheme of things. We live in a decade that is rediscovering tradition in architecture, and with it we seem poised to reinvest buildings with more humane values than they have recently known. Ornament, for example, of a historical sort, is slowly finding its way back to the American city. It may once again help us to make sense of institutional sameness by generating styles in architecture that make buildings type-specific—one iteration for schools, another for churches, and so forth. It may help to please us through the inclusion of archetypal parts charged with symbolic meanings we can understand. And it may once again allow us to have the pleasure of inhabiting buildings demonstrably made by humans, wherein there is something carved, sculpted, painted, woven, smoothed, or fashioned by the human hand, precious because unrepeatable.

Index